C000008653

Robert Taylor Pritchett

Rambles and Scrambles in Norway

Robert Taylor Pritchett

Rambles and Scrambles in Norway

ISBN/EAN: 9783337727482

Printed in Europe, USA, Canada, Australia, Japan

Cover: Foto ©ninafisch / pixelio.de

More available books at **www.hansebooks.com**

RAMBLES AND SCRAMBLES

IN

NORWAY

By ROBERT TAYLOR PRITCHETT

WITH MORE THAN ONE HUNDRED AND TWENTY ILLUSTRATIONS

LONDON
VIRTUE & CO., LIMITED, 26, IVY LANE
PATERNOSTER ROW
1879

PREFACE.

THE object of the present work is to bring before the notice of the general reader and tourist the advantages and pleasure accruing from a few weeks' sojourn among the mountains and fjords of that grand yet simple country, Norway. Everywhere abounding with features of interest, it will especially commend itself to the Englishman when he calls to mind how close was the link between the Scandinavians and his ancestors.

To travel profitably it is not sufficient merely to notice or admire scenic effects. Men and manners should also be closely observed; and no object or detail, however trivial, should be neglected or deemed beneath regard. Norway presents a wide field for observation and research, whatever may be the tastes and predilections of the visitor. Here may the geologist, if so disposed, find ample material for study; the archæologist and antiquarian may revel among Runic stones, Viking tumuli, rites and ceremonies, quaint wood-carvings adorned with the ever-twining serpent, costumes, customs, &c.; the keenest sportsman will find a treat in store for him; while the lover of the grand in nature and of simple rustic life will meet with them here to his heart's content. But to do this the main roads and cities must be abandoned for the mountains and fjelds, with their reindeer tracts and trout streams.

To the Fjeld, then, to the Fjeld! with its beautiful flora and mosses, its sport, its avalanches and landslips, its balmy air and soothing zephyrs. To the Fjeld—off to the Fjeld!

R. T. P.

CONTENTS.

LIST OF ILLUSTRATIONS.

— ◆

FULL-PAGE ILLUSTRATIONS.

ILLUSTRATIONS IN THE TEXT.

CHRISTIANSAND AND CHRISTIANIA.

CHRISTIANSAND AND CHRISTIANIA.

GAMLE NORGE—AN EARLY MURRAY—UNEXPLORED STATE OF THE COUNTRY—THE PIONEERS
OF SPORT—CROSSING THE NORTH SEA—NOT THEN AS NOW—CONTENT OF THE PEASANTS
—CHARM OF THE FIELD—CHRISTIANSAND—CHRISTIANIA—THE EMIGRANT'S VICISSITUDES
THE VICTORIA HOTEL AND OSCAR HALL.

Løvastrangene Fos.

OR comparatively few years has Norway received any attention from the travelling public. The beauty and grandeur of the country and the simple habits of the people were known to but few, and only heard of occasionally from some energetic salmon fisher who preferred outdoor life, good sport, plain food, and vigorous health to the constant whirl of advanced civilisation, busy cities, over-crowded *soirées*, high-pressure dinners, and the general hurry-skurry of modern life. The words "Gamle Norge," or old Norway, while exciting the greatest enthusiasm in Norway itself, rejoice the heart not only of many an Englishman who has become practically acquainted with its charms, but of those who, having heard of them, long to go and judge for themselves. Nor is the expression of modern introduction; it was evidently well known in the sixteenth century, as our immortal bard alludes to it in *Hamlet*.

Forty-five years ago Norway and its salmon fisheries were unknown luxuries. Even as late as 1839 Murray published a post-octavo Handbook

for Travellers in Denmark, Norway, and Sweden, in the preface to which
occur the subjoined passages :—

" The principal object of the following pages is to afford such of my
travelling countrymen as are disposed to quit the more beaten paths of
Southern Europe, and explore the less known, but equally romantic,
regions of the north, some useful information as to time and distance,
which at present they can only obtain by time and experience.   Beyond
Hamburg all is unknown land ; no guide-book contains any account of the
Baltic steamboats, still less of the means of travelling, either by land or
water, in the more distant lands of Norway and Sweden.   At the steam-
packet offices in London you may learn that an English steamer sails three
times a month from Lubec to Stockholm, but no further information can
be obtained.

*   *   *   *

" Unless the weather is unusually stormy, and the passage of the vessel
has consequently been delayed, the steamer remains in the outer harbour,
called Klippen, for four or five hours ; enabling the passengers who are
going straight to Norway to inspect the city, which is well worth seeing.
A miniature steamboat, the smallest I have ever seen, conveys you from
the quay, at which the larger vessel remains moored, up the long harbour
to the town itself, the journey occupying about half-an-hour.   In the
afternoon the *Constitution* continues her voyage, stretching much further
out to sea, in crossing the Skager Rack, until, at an early hour the next
morning, you reach Frederiksværn, the principal arsenal of Norway, situated
at the entrance of the winding fjord of Christiania.   From this place a
smaller coasting steamboat conveys the passengers to Christiania, touching,
in its passage up the Christiania fjord, at the various small towns and
villages on either shore.

*   *   *   *

" Steam vessels have for the last two or three years plied between
Christiania and Frederiksværn and Bergen, but their times of leaving have
hitherto been very irregular ; beyond Bergen I am not aware that any
regular communication has hitherto been projected.

*   *   *   *

"No traveller has any business to intrude among the mountain fast-nesses of Norway, unless he can not only endure a fair proportion of bodily fatigue, but can likewise put up with accommodations of the coarsest description. As far as Christiania this, of course, does not apply: the transport thither is by a comfortable steamboat, and the Hôtel du Nord sufficiently good to satisfy any man; but when you attempt to penetrate into the bowels of the land the case is different.

    *   *   *   *

"The Norsemen are strict Lutherans; scarcely an individual is to be met with professing any other creed, and no place of worship of any other kind exists in Norway. No Jew is allowed to set foot in Norway—a strange law in this free country. It has often struck me as a curious anomaly, that in the free cities of the Continent these unhappy outcasts were far worse treated than under many despotic governments. Commercial jealousy in a great measure accounts for this enmity in a city of merchants, but in a poor and thinly-populated country like Norway this motive could have no weight. I have been unable to learn from what cause the exclusion originated, though it is said to have originated from some idle fear that they would possess themselves of the produce of the silver mines at Kongs-berg; but it is certainly a most startling fact that the freest people on earth should cling with such watchful jealousy to one of the most illiberal and inhuman laws that can be conceived."

Soon after this our real sport-lovers began to discover the charms of Norway, Sir Hyde Parker, Sir Richard Sutton, and Lionel James leading the van; and within the space of forty years the transition has taken place from free fishing and shooting to the Scotch system of letting moors—a state of things that would astonish Forrester and Biddulph, whose work on Norway has now become historical and of the greatest interest. Forrester begins thus (A.D. 1834):—"Eight days in the North Sea, beating against foul winds, or, which was still worse, becalmed amongst fleets of Dutch fishing-boats, and ending in a regular gale of wind, which was worst of all, prepared us to hail the sight of land, and that of the coast of Norway." This passage was made in a little Norwegian schooner, bound from Gravesend to the south of Norway.

How different is it now! Thanks to Messrs. Wilson, steamers take us thither almost to the hour, unless, indeed, the clerk of the weather should connive with old Neptune to teach us a lesson, by reminding us that the elements are not yet to be ordered about entirely as we like. English visitors commenced about 1824; Lord Lothian, Lord Clanwilliam, and Lord H. Kerr, 1827; Marquis of Hastings, 1829; and in 1830 we have Elliott's account of Norway. Those were early days, when the *bønder* were astonished, and could hardly believe their own eyes, when Englishmen went down with a piece of thread and a kind of coach-whip to kill a salmon of thirty pounds; or, again, when the first flying shot opened a new world to them. Those were the times when members of the Storthing (or Parliament) appeared in the costume of their own district, with belts, tolle-knives, &c. They were not so eager to grasp at civilisation as the Japanese, who simultaneously took to elastic boots, tall black hats, and the English language within a year. No; they are a contented people, with no desire for change, or to have it thrust upon them, until they discover that they can make money of the delighted foreigner, who, elevated by the grandeur of the mountain scenery, grows more warm-hearted, kind, and generous than ever. Then the Norseman becomes rabid and exacting; but the provinces (thank Heaven!) still preserve their primitive simplicity.

Let us, then, hasten to these happy hunting-grounds. The fjeld life will blow all the smoke out of us, and if we love nature we can store up health and purity of thought, and bring back concentrated food for happy reflection, should we be spared to a good old age. How such reminiscences will then come out, brightened by the fact that all the petty *désagréments* of travel have been forgotten as they receded in the past! We need not enlarge on the pleasures of anticipation, the punctual meeting at the railway station, the satisfaction of knowing that nothing has been omitted or left behind—a congratulation sometimes a little blighted by the discovery that some one, after ransacking everything, cannot find his breech-loader or cartridge cases, or that some one else has left his pet "butchers" or "blue doctors" on his dressing-table. Should such mischances occur, they are soon dissipated in the general atmosphere of enjoyment and anticipation, assisted by the thought that it is of no use losing one's temper, as it is sure to be found again, and the temporary loss of it grieves one's friends unnecessarily, to say nothing of personal discomfort. Happy thought—always leave your ill-temper at home; or, better still, do not have one: it is not a home comfort.

The first port touched *en route* for the capital of Norway is Christiansand, which is snugly hidden in the extreme south of the district of Sætersdalen—that land of eccentricity in costume and quaintness of habitation, of short waists and long trousers reaching to the shoulders,

Christiansand.

above which come the shallow, baby-looking jackets. With what zest does one strain for the first peep at a seaport of a foreign land! What value is attached to the earliest indication of varying costume, or even a new form of chimney! The steamer from Hull generally arrives at Christiansand on Sunday, when it is looking its neatest, the white tower of the church shining over the wooden houses of the town, the Norwegian shipping all in repose, with the exception, perhaps, of the heavy, compressed, Noah's ark kind of dumpy barges, or a customs' gig containing some official. As we looked up at the church tower we could not but wonder if we should hear, during our short visit, the whistle of the "Vægter;" for tradition says that, for the protection of the place, a watchman is always on the look-out, ready to give the alarm should a fire break out in the town, which, being built almost entirely of wood, would soon be reduced to a heap of ashes. But no; we heard no whistle, not even a rehearsal. *On dit* that for three hundred years has the Vægter looked out afar, and no alarum has issued from the tower. Christiansand has been mercifully preserved from fire, and long may it be so!

During the passage over a friend told me of a Norwegian he once met on board. He was a Christiansander. The Norseman was in high glee, and, having entered into conversation with my friend, soon proposed a *skaal* (health). This achieved, the story of the Norseman began to run rapidly off the reel, and it is so characteristic of the people that we cannot do better than repeat it here. Born at Christiansand, at the age of sixteen Lars became restless, wanted to see America, and make his way in life, for which there was not much scope in the small seaport. Lars's father and mother were then living, with one daughter, who would take care of them whilst he started for the battle-field of life. He therefore determined to go. On his arrival in America he had a terrible struggle for existence, there being so many emigrants of all nations and classes. After patient endurance he began to get on, and saved sufficient to go to Chicago and California. During this time of trial how he thought about the chimes from the old white tower, the Vægter, and the fair-haired sister he had left behind, and wondered if all were well with the old people! At San Francisco he did pretty well for some time; but hearing one day that at Yokohama, in Japan, there was a good opening for a supply of butter (*smör*), his Norske associations were aroused, and his thoughts ran back to *sæters, piger*, cows, cream, and green pastures. That was the thing for Lars. So off he started for Yokohama, and having established a lucrative butter business, he determined to write home and send some money to his father and mother. This was a great pleasure to the kind-hearted fellow, while their answer assured him of the joy of those whom he had left behind on hearing of his safety and success, and receiving such a token of filial love. But the associations of home and childhood are strong, and it was not long before he experienced a desire to return. At length, however, he decided on developing the butter trade still further, and then, having a good offer to go back to San Francisco, he sold the whole business and good-will for a good round sum, and started on a new career, which this time took the form of brewing. How Norwegian! what national items!—butter (*smör*) and ale (*öl*). Again Lars was successful, and derived much comfort from the fact that he was thereby enabled to enhance the home happiness at Christiansand. Happy the son who comforts a father! Happy the paternal old age cherished by a son's love! Beer, or rather ale, became the basis of a lucrative business. Lars, however, speedily discovered that bottled ale was the leading article to make the concern pay largely. But bottles were the difficulty; they were expensive items, and not manufactured in San Francisco. Lars often thought over this problem, which his partner, likewise, was unable to solve. Luckily one evening the good Norseman—he must have been indulging in a quiet pipe —had a happy thought. While musing over his early days the bottle-makers of Christiansand passed before him. He at once decided on making arrangements for visiting the old seaport, and, having seen those most dear to him on earth, to bring a bottle manufacturer back with him, thus combining business with pleasure. This is the yarn he told my friend, and when they entered the harbour poor Lars's anxiety was intense. He had telegraphed to say that he was coming, and expected some one to meet and welcome him. During his absence he had heard that his sister had married happily, and that the son-in-law was very kind to his father; so Lars's mind was set at rest. A boat neared the steamer, in the stern-sheets of which sat an aged man, a fair-haired Norseman rowing him. The old man was Lars's father, who was soon on deck looking round, but he could not see his boy. At last, however, he spied him, and, throwing his arms round his neck, was fairly overcome with joy. On recovering, the old gentleman began a good flow of Norske, when poor Lars for the first time realised how long he had been away; for, like the Claimant, he could not remember his native language, and it was some time before either of them thought of landing. Meanwhile, we heartily wish the good Lars increased success. May his bottles be manufactured on the spot, and his good øl cheer the heart without muddling the brain!

When we entered Christiansand we also looked out for a boat; for Hans Luther Jordhoy had come down from Gudbransdalen to meet us, and was soon on board. A closely knit frame, fair beard, moderate stature, and kindly eye—there stood our future companion before us. Our first impressions were never disturbed; he had very good points, and has afforded us many pleasing associations in connection with our visit to Norge.

As we steamed out of the harbour of Christiansand we met a passenger coast steamer coming in—one of those innumerable small screw steamers which run in and out of every fjord from Cape Lindesnæs to the North Cape. Are their names not written in *Norges Communicationer*, the Norwegian *Bradshaw?* The kindly feeling of the Norwegians towards the English was at once manifest, for no sooner did the brass band on board the excursion boat recognise our nationality than it struck up "God save the Queen." We quite regretted that we had no band to return the compliment, and the only thing left for us was to give them a hearty cheer.

This done, we started on our run to Christiania, with comparatively smooth water, a lovely evening, a prolonged *crepusculum*, and, late in the evening, a sweet little French song, sung with the most delightful simplicity by a lady. "Petites Fleurs des Bois" is indelibly impressed on the mind of the Patriarch. When it afterwards became known that we were indebted to an English bride for such a treat—which it really was—the bachelors whispered "A happy bond of union!" but considered, at the same time, that Norwegian travelling was scarcely made on purpose for honeymooning. Take carrioles, for instance, or the jolting *stolkjærre*, in which the bride might sometimes find herself unceremoniously thrown into the lap of the bridegroom, or *vice versâ*. No; unless the lady is familiar with the manners, customs, and petty inconveniences attendant on travelling in Norway, that country will not prove the happy hunting-ground for honeymoons.

The Courtyard, Victoria Hotel, Christiania.

The whole of the Christiania fjord is both grand and immense. A decided flutter takes place on board when the town is in sight, and preparations are made for disembarkation. Hans Luther had by this time made a personal acquaintance with our luggage, and went to the Custom House, whither we were soon sent for. Among our possessions were discovered certain condiments and preserved provisions unknown to the officials, one item especially—pea soup in powder. On our arrival we suggested that the unusual product should be tasted. To this the official at first demurred, but ultimately yielded. Unfortunately, at the very moment of putting the powder to his lips, he drew a long breath, which sent the dry powdered pea soup down the wrong way. However, after a time he recovered, when doubtlessly he registered a mental vow never, never again to taste any foreign importation.

We were soon at the Victoria Hotel, with its quaint courtyard, with galleries running round it, excessively tame pigeons hopping and perching on all sides, and a reindeer head nailed to the woodwork. During the tourist season a large marquee is erected in the centre of this courtyard for *tables d'hôte* and extra meals. In the meantime we hurried to our rooms, longing to be out in a boat for a general view of the city. A few extras were, however, requisite before starting in real earnest, amongst which were two rifle slings. These had to be made, and are referred to here because they were the means of initiating us into one of the customs of the place. The leather slings were well made, but the price was most *tolly* (exorbitant). This led to a mild remonstrance, upon which the saddler wrote us a remarkable letter, which it is a pity we cannot present *verlatim*. It was to the effect that the saddler was happy to serve us well, but thinking we were English gentlemen, he imagined we should prefer giving English prices. However, if we merely wished to pay in accordance with the Norwegian tariff, it would only be so much, which was precisely the amount we did pay.

Christiania has a population of about seventy thousand, and owes its modern appearance to the destruction of the old town by fire. Nowadays the suburbs extend widely all round it, while to the westward villas reach almost to Oscar's Hall, an object of interest distinctly visible both from the town and the fortress, being only about four miles distant by land, and half that amount by water. The villa, with its high tower, is the property of the King, and is rich in the native talent of Tidemand, who was the national genre painter of his day. There are magnificent views of the fjord, bay, and surrounding mountains from all points, whether high or low, from the fortress or from the Egeberg, from the tower of the church in the market-place, or, farther off, from the

Christiania.

Frogner Sæter and the Skougemsaas. For the latter, however, a long day should be taken.

To visit Oscar's Hall the most pleasant way is to take a boat and row across. This was suggested by Hans, and we were glad to find that he took kindly to boat work, as he came from Gudbransdalen, which is inland. More pleased, however, were we to discover, when about half-way across, that Hans was gradually bursting out into song, singing in a clear voice one of Kjerulf's sweetest compositions, which we give in part at the end of the chapter. There is a plaintive sweetness throughout it, and the beauty of the evening, coupled with the surprise, caused us to anticipate

A Timber Shoot.

many future repetitions, as nothing, when travelling, is more humanising and soothing than vocal or instrumental music.

The University, the Storthing, museums, and Mr. Bennett have already been frequently described: still just one word. Every Englishman is received by Mr. Bennett, who carries out his slightest wish. We only called to see him, and get some *smarpenge;* for if we had not, no one would have believed that we had been to Norway. Before the country was well opened Mr. Bennett must have been of the greatest service to visitors.

During our very short stay we had an excellent opportunity of judging of the character of the people when collected in masses. There were to be a great procession of guilds and all kinds of things at the New Palace. These we attended, and very gratified we were to find how orderly the good folk were; how quiet, and yet with what a sense of comfortable enjoyment, if we may use the term; no excitement, but a cheerful interest in all that was going on; no crushing, no rush of roughs. If such were the case in large towns, we considered it augured well for the provinces.

Between Christiania and Kongsberg much timber is seen wending its way down to the fjord. An instance of a *timber jam* after a shoot is given in the accompanying illustration. Sometimes trees are torn away at flood-time. The regular timber is duly marked and started, and at certain periods of the year persons follow the course of the river for the purpose of releasing the *jams* and helping the timber on its way to Drammen, where it is shipped for all parts of the world.

Little is said here of the cities of Christiania, Bergen, and Trondhjem, as our path lies in the open, the fjeld life, *sæters*, peasants, and sport. Our delight is to live out of the present century in fresh air and simplicity, where trolds might cross our path, where we might see the lovely Huldre, the beauty who had the unfortunate appendage of a cow's tail, which, when exposed to view, was the signal for her to vanish into thin air, or where Odin and Thor had had great *jagt*, and killed bears, elks, gluttons, and wolves. The scenes we longed for were those in which pagan rites had been carried out with all the grandeur of mighty warriors and priests worthy of Valhalla; wherein Vikings, after deeds of valour, were laid low, and buried with great solemnity and becoming pomp in their own war vessels, with their treasure, their arms, and their hunting-gear about them, waiting for the call to glory.

INGRIDS VISE.

REINDYR CHORUS.

Music by H. KJERULF.   Words by BJÖRNSON.

THELEMARKEN.

THELEMARKEN.

HELEMARKEN is a large district, lying in the south-east of Norway, north of Sæters-dalen, which is the most southern part of the kingdom. It is characterized by forest, costume, and wood-carving, the latter being applied on a large scale to the external decoration of houses, and especially to the storehouse, which is always a separate building of one story, and locally called the *stabur*. On the exterior of this structure is lavished all the carving talent and energy of the proprietor and his friends; while inside will be found good old coffers, containing the silver and the tankards, the brooches and the bridal crown, which is handed down from generation to generation amongst the *bönder*, or farmers. A public parochial crown is sometimes to be heard of, and may be seen at the lawyer's, for that profession is known in Norway; and, when litigation commences, it is impossible to guess the time over which it may extend. But to return to wood-carving, so important a feature in the dwellings of the inhabitants of this part,

A fine specimen of carved lintel, or side-post, is in existence near Lysthus, displaying wonderful solidity, and a flowing Runic design extremely difficult to copy. How was it originated? What was the *motif* of the design? After making a careful study of it, it appears to be the result of "eyes"—generally associated without hooks—being kept to

Norwegian Carved Lintels.

themselves, and interlaced, one following the other. On trying this, it was found to be practicable and most successful. Talking over this glorious old work with the good housewife, she called her husband, who went off to the *stabur*, and, quickly returning, told me there was a very old and handsome pair of these lintels lying under the "provision house," and begged me to accept them in recollection of my visit, and take them back

to my own home, that they might give me pleasure there. Great was my
wish to accept them, but the difficulty of transit soon flashed across my
mind. Our route lay over the Haukelid, with hours of snow—ponies
sinking in, and perhaps through. So the transit being impossible, I
tendered my thanks for the kindly offer. It was with much regret that I
did so, but what could be done hundreds of miles from home, and just
starting over the roughest mountain tracts to the north-west of Norway?
Nothing but a grateful negative, and a suggestion that they should be

Carved House in Thelemarken.

given to the next nice young couple who were starting housekeeping.
The principal carving, as we have already observed, is lavished on the
storehouses; and as soon as a loving couple are engaged, the man begins
to build his nest, with nothing much but his axe for strong work and a
knife for ornamentation. The latter instrument is most adroitly used by
the peasants, cutting all sweeping curves, with the left-hand thumb used
as a lever. The house-building is characterized by large timbers squared,
afterwards calked with moss, and the ends crossing. As will be hereafter
shown, the timbers are generally numbered externally up to twelve, so that

they may be easily rebuilt should occasion arise to remove the house
elsewhere. Looking at these immense solid timbers, what a contrast
they present to modern work; how like their sturdy forefathers, who
worked so solidly; how unlike the feather-edged boarding of the new half-
civilised houses which are now being introduced near towns, and are
flimsiness itself, and only carpenter's shoddy!

Kongsberg is a city of rushing waters, or rather a small town; and
approaching it is suggestive of proximity to a seltzer-water bottle with
the cork partially out. The river rushes, splutters, fumes, foams, and

Carved Houses, Bru, Thelemarken.

steams; huge sticks, fir poles, and stems battling their way down the
broken waters to Drammen, preparatory to their being shipped for the
warmer and drier sphere of civilisation and circular saws. Some three
English miles below Kongsberg is the Labro Fos, which is very interesting, and well worth visiting, inasmuch as it affords an admirable opportunity of seeing the timber shoot the Fos—large fir-stems sometimes
coming clean over the fall into the roar below.

Kongsberg is a centre of interest, as close by are found the silver
mines which have for ages supplied the raw material for the *gamle
sölv,* such as silver crowns, belts, cups, tankards, and all the endless

Kongsberg : Thelemarken.

variety of ornament for which Gamle Norge has been, and is, so famous.
However, we will not now enter into this subject, but will merely mention
that interesting specimens of this class of work are to be found in England,
souvenirs of travel which are highly prized by the happy possessors and
their friends also. The silver is not considered very pure, but the old
designs are very grand and admirable. The modern specimens, and
especially those in filigree, are far inferior, being poor in design and
unsubstantial.

Forests are most typical of Thelemarken, and very suggestive of bears
in winter, a season much more severe here than in some other parts of
Norway, as the district is away east, beyond the influence of the gulf-
stream. It is a curious fact that directly an Englishman arrives in
Thelemarken everybody seems to have seen bears, or, to be more precise,
to have had visions of bears. That there are bears is certain. A sport-
loving Oxonian last year was disappointed of a bear in the north, and,
coming south on his return to shoot blackcock, had lighted his pipe and
was walking quietly back when he saw a bear! He was seventy yards off,
and had only one cartridge. He fired. Bruin, falling back on his
haunches, put out his "embracers," and rushed forward for the "hug,"
when he gave a roll and fell backwards—dead. He was a splendid beast,
judging from the skin. What a trophy to bring home! "What luck!"
some said. On his return, the fortunate hunter—who, by-the-bye, was a
week later than he should have been—heard the momentous words from
his dear parent, "Well, sir, where is the bear you went out to shoot in
Norway?" "Have you not seen it? It's in the hall." "Oh, my dear
boy, I am so delighted—so glad! Come, let us have the skin up here.
Send for mamma. This is capital!" How much nicer it is to bring
home a bear-skin than to have to say, "Didn't shoot one!" Who does
not know what zest there always is in success?

The costume of the district is worn in every-day life, by the farmers as
well as the peasants; in fact, the farmers, or *bönder*, are very proud of
their dress. First and foremost is the typical white jacket, with light blue
facings and silver buttons; blue collars, blue pocket flaps, with silver
buttons also; the jacket turned well back, with a light blue *revers*, as

I think the ladies call it. But the great characteristic of the jacket is not to be too long; the *ton* only have the back to come down just below the shoulder-blade; and, as the black trousers rush up to meet the curtailed garment, one can imagine the vast area of black trouser before arriving at the foot of the figure; it really makes them all look out of drawing.

The women wear a chocolate-coloured handkerchief cleverly twisted round the head and falling down the back, with the hair plaited; and well they look with their fair hair and ribbons, their homespun or *vadmel* petticoats closely kilt-plaited, old silver brooches and studs, and sometimes silk handkerchiefs as aprons, with coloured cinctures, the bodice with dark ground and flowers, crewel-worked, in relief. Near Lysthus the costume is nearly all blue, a kind of short frock-coat, with dark blue trouser-gaiters, embroidered up the side with yellow and scarlet; but this is not a successful phase of costume.

On Sunday every variety is seen, and the additional interest of lake travelling is met with—namely, the raft boats, consisting of seven stems of trees, the longest in the middle, the six cut shorter, like organ pipes; midships a seat for one; while the oars are tied in with green birch twigs with the leaves on. How suggestive of early lake habitation, and yet how like a modern outrigger; for there is only room for one and a *fine*, or provision box, from which a Norwegian, male or female, is inseparable.

The shortness of the jackets is shown in an illustration which represents a custom peculiar to this part, namely, smoking the cows (see p. 36). Many travellers have complained of the flies in Norway, and now even Norwegian cows object to them, and the farm folk, in kindly sympathy, make fires of juniper, the smoke of which is unwelcome to the mosquitoes. Into this smoke the cows are only too glad to go, and being well flavoured with juniper, are ready to start forth for the day, regardless of their little winged enemies. We speak from practical experience when we add that the traveller likewise will be rather benefited by participating in the process.

Here, perhaps, it would be as well to refer to the hour-glass under the initial letter at the commencement of the chapter. It is composed of brass, and placed by the side of the pulpit, which is opposite to the King's pew or box in the church at Kongsberg. There are four hour-glasses— quarter, half, three-quarters, and hour; so the domine, or minister, turns the glass before commencing his discourse, and the congregation knows how long he will continue. At Tönsberg there is a curious mural historical souvenir, consisting of the top of a stool let into the wall, on which may be read the following:—

"In the year 1589, being the 11th day of November, came the well-

The Raft Boat: Thelemarken.

born gentleman, Mr. Jacobus Stuart, King of Scotland: and the 25th Sunday after Trinity, which was the 16th day of November, he sat on this stool and heard a preaching from the 23rd Psalm, 'The Lord is my Shepherd.' Mr. David Lentz preached, and he preached between 10 and 12."

This "well-born gentleman" was evidently James the First of England and Sixth of Scotland, who married Anne of Denmark, sister of Christian IV.

Leaving Lysthus, we settled down for steady travelling in that most delightful style, namely, with our tents and luggage, sometimes in a *stolkjær*, or country cart, sometimes with ponies only. Such independence, such health-giving enjoyment, can hardly be obtained under different circumstances. The travellers in this case were three, happily organized in the following manner. They might for the nonce be called Brown, Jones, and Robinson, as a tribute of respect to the originals in the "Primer or Spelling Book," published in 1790, where those now world-known names are first found associated. Let us rather go with the times, and number them—a treatment now general in hotels, both at home and abroad.

So, to commence, No. 1 was the youngest, and unanimously elected Paymaster-general. Polyglot in his knowledge of languages, he shone when asked to explain: then came such volleys of Norske, German, Danish, Swedish, French, Italian, all in one flowing Norskey catena, that, if people did not understand them, they felt they ought to, and acted accordingly. All this was carried out with the dash of a Zouave, and garnished with a profound knowledge of music and brilliant execution on the piano. How we longed sometimes for a pocket piano! No. 1's great *forte* was enthusiasm for fishing—trout, salmon, greyling, and split-cane fly-rods. Tradition says that he has often in his sleep talked of "blue doctors," "large butchers," and "black doses," these sounds having been heard in the small hours of the morning zephyring from his tent with nasal accompaniments; but he was always equal to the occasion, even when some one had landed with the luggage by mistake. "Never mind, my dear boy; sure to find it; most honest, charming people, these Norwegians—never lose anything." Such were the comforting words which emanated from No. 1 when he understood that No. 3 had lost his luggage; but when he found that it was his own a change came over the spirit of his dream. The polyglot vocabulary was soon launched, the fire of the Zouave flared up, a carriole was ordered, and the pursuit commenced, which happily ended in the recovery of the wandering impedimenta, when Richard became himself again.

No. 2 was Tentmaster-general, and a sportsman to the core. Reindeer, salmon, and Gamle Norge—these he had chronically on the

Hitterled Church : Sunday Morning.

brain, mixed up with a great love of old tankards and a yearning for silver belts and *gammelt sølv.* Once in his Norfolk jacket and knickers, *pua de höie fjelde,* how happy was he! rejoicing in the *friske luft,* mountain air, and snow peaks (*snebræer*), ready for any amount of fatigue, and always willing to cook first and eat afterwards. A rare good man was the Tentmaster.

No. 3 was generally known as "the Locust," from his constant appetite for all kinds of food, and general thirst for knowledge about everything connected with Norway. Note-book in hand, he was ever jotting down everything, even to catching mosquitoes between the leaves of it, so as to bring home the real thing. Still No. 3 had an important duty to perform. As the travellers were three, he was allowed the casting vote—a most wholesome arrangement, as he was a married man, and consequently likely to be useful in some weighty matters. Happily, to the credit of No. 1 and No. 2, the exercise of No. 3's prerogative was never called for, and by the end of the trip was looked on as a sinecure. Still he always travelled ready to apply "a touch of the oil feather"—one of the best companions a traveller can have ready to hand. May many such trios have a trip of such great yet simple enjoyment, such health, and such pleasing diversion of thought! It is a joy to fall back upon throughout life, and the longer the life the greater the relish of recollection.

Hitterdal Church is one of the two wooden churches of which Norway can boast, the other being that of Borgund. They are built of wood, Byzantine-Gothic, *on dit,* but grotesque and pagodaist in form. The old porches are grandly carved with serpents, dragons, and Runic interlacings. The church itself at Hitterdal is nothing like so quaint or picturesque as that at Borgund, neither is it so weird; still, its early carving forms a noble monument to come down to us, and at once draws forth the admiration, not only of the antiquarian, but of the casual passer-by. The lintels at the entrance are especially beautiful. The bell-tower is unusually detached, in this case being placed on the other side of the highway. Unfortunately, time prevented a more detailed sketch of the old chair or seat given on page 29: it stands in the church by the altar, and is considered episcopal, but the date is most likely *circa* 900. What grand

solidity of form! Vikingly to a degree, and fit for Thor or Odin.   There
is a great air of majesty about it.

The roof of the church is also of wood, carved in the same way as
many of the churches in Sussex, and covered with small wooden tiles,

Porch at Hitterdal: Thelemarken.

if that term may be used to describe the process which in that county is
generally known as "shingling."

The churchyard is very interesting, and the grave-boards have a
peculiar form worthy of notice; for this reason one is introduced here.
The shape of the upper part is that of a cross, but below come up
two horns, rising right and left.   These horns have a kind of anchor
form; and what could be a more appropriate emblem in a country so

sea-bound as Norge? The blending of Faith and Hope is, I think, most poetically suggested. Can we do better here than pay a tribute of respect to the beautiful simplicity of the religious character of the Norwegian peasantry? Their love of God and their reverence for religion are refreshing, and offer a good lesson to many who rejoice in mere flourish of external worship. We shall have occasion to refer to the curious anomaly of Roman Catholic vestments continued in the present day in the Lutheran service, but allusion may now be made to the happy link which exists between the ministers and people. This is shown in the

Chair in Hitterdal Church.

character of the sermons, the whole tone of which seems to aim at binding the parish together in Christian love and sympathy, bearing each other's burdens, caring for one another, and curbing self—the most difficult of all tasks, as it comes nearest home, and is in itself so antagonistic to the inclinations of human nature. The whole climate rather tends to develop this frame of mind: there is a certain sedate expression throughout the provinces: the long darkness of winter, extending its influence even into the continuous light of the northern summer, brings every one into close and constant proximity, whilst the mountains isolate the valleys one from the other without any access. Still, when the summer comes and the whole energy of vegetation bursts out at once, how their gladdened hearts rejoice! They pluck these outbursts of beauty and revived nature, and joyously take them to the house of God—no mere form or ritual, but the wholesome outcome of heartfelt, unsophisticated joy and gratitude for brightness after lengthened gloom and months of pent-up feeling.

Leaving Hitterdal, we were off in earnest for the Hardanger, with a grand country before us. The first night we pulled up at Skeje. Before coming to our resting-place at the end of the lake, we noticed the saw-mills and corn-mills (seven, one above the other); not that torrents are scarce in Norway, but in this valley there was employment. Arrived at Skeje, our Tentmaster having selected his spot, tents were pitched, and everything put ship-shape for the night. The only milk we could get was goat's milk, and *fladbröd* in abundance. It is, perhaps, superfluous to mention here that *fladbröd* can be made very toothsome by drying it before the fire : the peasants keep it in a state ready for travelling, with the means of folding it up so as not to be shaken into dust by the jolting of the *stolkjær*, which certainly would be the case had it been fit for eating. The smoke of our fire had gone up, and after our meal and a chat with our neighbours we turned in. A strange dog came into the Patriarch's tent, and eventually curled himself up for the night, and, as a mark of gratitude for welcome, woke him in the morning by licking his face.

Next day brought us on to Flatdal. Looking over that grand, deep valley, we halted awhile at a picturesque wooden house : we asked for milk, which was brought forthwith, and it was goat's milk. The daughter, as it was Saturday afternoon, was engaged plaiting her two long tails ready for the morrow. The good mother had a very fine antique silver brooch, and the proprietor one also on his shirt-front, and after we had drunk our milk they showed us their rooms, which were most interesting, and dated very far back ; for traces of the fact presented themselves on all sides, especially in the harness and elaborately carved horse-collars, which bore the crest of a lion's head on an escutcheon—evidently belonging to the days of aristocratic Norway.

Flatdal : Thelemarken.

We had bivouacked on a green lawn near the village, close to a house which was a carriole station. Our three tents were a novelty, and our cooking at last brought a crowd around us; but we must say that the people were most kindly and considerate towards us. They had never seen such a thing before, and hated *fanter*, tinkers, and gipsies, which nearly included all wanderers in tents: such latter were we.

Next we inspected the *loom*, where a daughter was hard at work. There were a fine old bed, with inscription, and many spinning-wheels, highly coloured (green, red, and blue and white, with black). It is a pity an illustration of this room cannot be given in colour. We descended into the *dal*: the heat was intense, no air below, and a pandemonium of flies. Bathing under the wheel of a mill was a temporary relief: our torment was renewed at lunch. But we were out to enjoy ourselves; so we did, in spite of mosquitoes. At lunch we cooked some of the trout our chief had killed *en route*, which that day numbered thirty. We were immensely amused here by noticing the very comic and inquiring expression in a magpie while listening, for the first time probably, to the English snore with which one of our party favoured us on this occasion, putting his head first on one side and then on the other, then taking a hop, and, when the music broke into a staccato bass passage, hopping back still more interested, until it finally flew off. Magpies are the sacred birds of the land, and are regarded as the private property of his Satanic Majesty.

After a long day and a mid-day meal, during which we were devoured by mosquitoes until nothing was left of us but our monograms, we arrived late in the evening in front of a farmhouse at Sillejord. It was Saturday night, and no room in the house, but an open space close by, most inviting for tents. In the twinkling of an eye the Tentmaster issued his order, each man had his tent laid out, and up they went simultaneously, to the astonishment of the natives. Was it a sort of fair, only read of in books? Was it the first germ of the great Russian fair of Nijni Novgorod? Was it one of the lost tribes of Israel come down from the clouds? Or were we Germans, who, having already annexed Denmark, had just run on with a message from Prince Bismarck to say that Norway also was

annexed? No; the peasants rather looked on at a respectful distance,
with a certain openness of mouth and absence of expression. By this
time, the tents being up, beds laid, saddle-bags in places, and guns hung
on tent-pole with telescope, food had to be thought of, and the canteen
business looked after. The canteen was well organized and an old
traveller—almost self-acting; so accustomed to the names of Fortnum
and Mason's tinned soups, &c., that the very words "mock-turtle" made
it burn and bristle up to a really good fire. That night we had good lake
trout; and how welcome, with our then appetites, the mock-turtle! Three
cheers for Fortnum and Mason! And then the *mörbradsteg!* Some of our
readers have never been introduced to those satisfying and necessary
pleasures of life; if not, let us explain. *Mörbradsteg* and other good
things in tins come from Stavanger in Norway, which is great in potted
meats, *ryper*, tins of all kinds of preserved things, soups, lobsters, &c., and
these *mörbrader*. The inquiring mind may ask, " But *mörbrader*—what is
it? how made?" All I can say is, that it was so good we thought we
had no time to ask what it was: perfect in flavour, solid in substance,
very satisfying to the most energetic of gastric juices, and wholesome.
Three cheers, therefore, for Stavanger! Then came wild strawberries,
brought by dear little children in costume, who had already begun to go
through the process of purification ready for Sunday, biscuits and Dutch
cheese, and a *skaal* for Gamle Norge. After this we followed the suggestion of the good motto, "Rest and be thankful," and then some
hunters' songs.

The following day (Sunday) was a curious scene; everybody came to
look at us. All the characteristics of national costume, as worn in
Thelemarken, were in full force. Let us first describe the *piger*, or girls.
They wear very short petticoats, and most becoming and picturesque they
are ; dark blue stockings with lovely clocks, and buckles on their shoes ;
the apron is embroidered with what now would be called crewel patterns
of flowers ; while a little below the waist is a rich many-coloured girdle,
ending in knobs of tassels of the brightest colours. The top of the
petticoat is bound with a bright colour, and shown, as the scarlet jacket,
which is frequent in this district, is as short as the men's, coming only a

little below the shoulder-blades. Tucked inside the girdle is generally seen a rich silk handkerchief, and in some cases two. The head-dress is another silk handkerchief, and into the tail of the back hair more colour is worked. On week days they wear large gaiters, like cloth trousers, which certainly attracted our attention when first seen.

Now for the lads of the village. They are not one tittle behind the girls in the pains they take as to their points, especially these—shortness of jacket, length of trouser, and brightness of colour. At Dabord they all adopted the shaven cheek, upper lip, and chin. The jacket is generally white, very short, as in Sætersdalen, just coming below the shoulder-blades: this curious garment is turned back at the cuffs and *revers* with light blue, the effect being heightened by silver buttons. The trousers are very curious—a fact necessitated by the shortness of the superstructure. The expanse of back is prodigious from the shoulder-blades downwards, they are wide in the leg, and generally have a stripe down the side. The short coatee affords a grand display of tolle-knives, the handles of which, in this part, are generally made of *lom* (maple), smooth, and uncarved, and deep in the sheath. In most cases they are suspended from a button, and not from a belt; in fact, belts are not of very frequent occurrence here. Skull-caps and hats are worn by the men, and the richest farmers maintain the national costume of the district. In some few instances for weddings the white jacket is daintily touched up with a little worked flower here and there on the edge and corner, which gives great finish. The clocks on the men's stockings are very rich: these are worn on fête days with breeches, which are worked in red and white round the buttons and up the seams. The garters are always objects of great taste and careful arrangement. It is when the holiday costumes are worn that the beautiful and mysterious Huldre appears, generally frequenting the mountains and forests, but sometimes joining in the festive dances of the mountaineers. When she vouchsafes this favour every young *bonde* is eager to dance with her—the handsome strange girl with the blue petticoat, and white handkerchief over her head. Tradition does not enlighten us much about this beauty, and the story of her sudden disappearance immediately her cow-tail is discovered is cruel.

F

Why does she come to Thelemarken, where the skirts are so short, sometimes only reaching the knee? If she be so fond of dancing, why not frequent country balls? Or she would be safer with a train of the present fashion; even if that were trodden on, her tail would be safe. Having noticed the general costume, let us enjoy the day of rest.

The brightness of the morning favoured our *al fresco* toilets, and one of our party (who carried a dressing-case full of wonderful things, and generally known in the list of impedimenta as "Somebody's luggage") became the centre of attraction. In front of his tent were laid out a waterproof sheet and a saddle-bag, partially opened and supported at the back; the latter sustained the looking-glass, in front of which knelt a figure shaving (No. 1). Now, although the Norwegians shave almost universally, there was something about our friend's manipulations which took the fancy of all present. The girls giggled; the short ones tried to peep between the tall ones. Why? Did the performer pull his own nose to a greater length than usual in this country when he took the long sweep down his cheek? Hardly. The fact was, the good folk thought the whole thing was but an overture to some other performance, and that the dressing-case, with its numerous silver-topped glass bottles, contained all kinds of medicines, panaceas for everything—cures for gout, sciatica, tic douloureux, trichinæ spirales, hypochondria, dipsomania, and every other mania.

After the shaving came a pause. A fortunate inquiry for old silver ornaments now changed the whole scene, and for the rest of the day, at intervals, the *penates* of the neighbourhood were being brought for our edification. Some of the old brooches were remarkably beautiful; the rings were very characteristic, some having small pendant rings, some with the usual cup ornaments; and when it was discovered that much interest was taken in old costumes, we had really a treat—embroideries on *vanter*, or winter gloves without fingers, eider-down cloaks, swaddling-bands, babies' caps, worked aprons, the open-work at the lower part being admirable in design. A wish was expressed to see a baby ready swaddled for baptism. Unhappily, there was no such thing to be had within miles upon miles; but rather than "the Locust" should be disappointed, these good people dressed up a woollen one, which

answered every purpose, and was considered a great success. The
kindness of the people was very striking; a certain shy curiosity
characterized their movements at first, but they soon settled down to
taking every possible pains to oblige us and meet our wants. It
seemed very odd, however, to see a church so near, and yet no service.
How was it, when we saw almost enough people to form a congregation?
It happened thus. The *prastegaard*, or clergyman's house, is at the
central church, which often has two or three *annexer*—small churches,
each eighteen or twenty miles from the principal one; the services,
therefore, are only held about every third Sunday in each church. Well
educated, well read, and, much like the old fathers, revered and well
beloved by their flocks, the clergy lead a hard life. The vast extent of
their parishes or districts is very trying to their health, necessitating
long drives, and in winter much severe sledge work; while on the
coast there is such boat work that the minister and doctor of the locality
seem more like "old salts" than members of those professions. I
remember particularly one clergyman, whose *annex* was on a group of
islands off the coast. As the steamer passed she swung round a point,
when a boat came off to us, with a grand figure standing up steering
her. From beneath an old sou'-wester streamed his white hair, grandly
blown back, and he wore silver spectacles, large muffler round his throat,
oilskin coat and trousers, and long sea boots. As the boat neared
the steamer and was turned to the gangway, a sailor on board
said, "Now, sir, you'll see one of the fine old sort; this, sir, is the
priest, and not a better seaman will you find all along the coast—nor a
better man." No wonder religion takes so simple and earnest a form
when its exponents practically exemplify, in their every-day life, its
sublime teachings with a simplicity, energy, and dignity far beyond the
conception of those working in densely populated districts; for the
priest, although but an occasional visitor to some parts, is a source of
comfort and sympathy to all in their trouble, and enters with the greatest
interest into their rejoicings and pleasures, whether they be public or
domestic. In this way their relations with their flocks are most "good
shepherd-like," and their constant care and solicitude for their parishioners

rivet the love and confidence of all around them. No doubt these
relations are materially assisted by the tolerably equal distribution of
this world's goods in spots remote from busy towns; or rather, to
speak more correctly, by the absence of wealth and the even-manneredness of all such Norwegian residents. Any stranger visiting Norway
will be struck with the large Elizabethan frill worn by the priest, which,
with the sombre black gown, and the two candlesticks constantly kept
on the altar ready to be lighted on three occasions— generally Christmas,

Smoking the Cows: Thelemarken.

the end of the forty days, and Easter—imparts a very mediæval
character to the service. All that we have here said of the relations
of the clergy with their congregations is abundantly confirmed by the
homely way in which the former give out the notices from the altar as
to the working of the parish or the schools, or any extra communion,
when requested by any of the parishioners.

Going to Berge from Sillejord, we had torrents of rain—a deluge:
we now approached higher ground and a blacker country. Snow ploughs
on the side of the road told tales of wintry difficulty of transit, while

Framigaard Louise.

sledges were round most of the houses. Arrived at the station, we found one small bedroom with strong store-closet atmosphere, game lost, &c. In the *vand* are perch; in the river, greyling. The hunter and *bonde* here was building a large room, which, though still unfinished, we decided to sleep in. We soon had a roaring fire; the beds were made, the Patriarch slinging his hammock under a huge carpenter's bench; then came the cooking, followed by a few songs; and finally stories of bears, wolves, wild cats, and lynxes from the *bonde*. There was a very fine old *mangletræ* here, two feet long. So peculiar an instrument of Norwegian household necessity is deserving of explanation : it is two feet long and four inches wide: B represents the things to be mangled ; c the roller; the right hand of the mangler takes hold of the lion at D, and the left hand on A balances the *mangletræ*, which is worked backwards and forwards until the things are done. *Mem.*—Last night

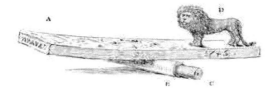

reindeer were seen above here ; and at the *vand*, high over this place, the *bonde* had seen a glutton after a wounded or sick reindeer. The chief brought in three trout for breakfast. Now the real life was bursting on us. How we drank in the stories of the hunter, rising in the morning to delight in the health and beauties about us!

At Mogen we found more signs of winter—sledges abundant, and one pigsty kind of hut surmounted by a wonderful group: snow shoes, old reindeer horns and heads, sledges, and a plough.* This is primitive: but it is not all: there were the old querns, or *haandkværn*. In spite of this we had not shaken the influence of travelling civilisation; the *bonde* asked us if we would like some "Bockley and Pukking's black-brown beer." Certainly. "Men hvor meget ?" Two and sixpence per bottle: it had been left by an Englishman. Eheu, what an anomaly!

---

* The iron of this plough is exactly the same as the hand-plough, or "casarhome," used in the Western Highlands, and now fast disappearing.

JAMSGAARD.—This was such an evening: north wind strong, bad for tents; large lawn discovered, camp inside; camp beds fitted up, cooking outside. The hammock was slung. How the north wind whistled, until we barricaded that side with hay! Then we all slept. In the morning we were to start early, and the perfect dignity with which the page entered the dormitory, with coffee for all, was truly a picture. We got a very good pony here, a true *bakken*, with black-centred hog mane, and zebra-marked legs, and started in lovely weather by the crystally clear Totak Vand, where we saw a large white owl; then to the larger Toftland, and on to Botten. We are now in snow-shoe land, with spills of birch-wood for pipes, and more mills, one over the other, for grinding. Grouge Kirk was interesting; and we saw a woman rowing over with homespun, to be sent to some commercial centre. Starting in a *stolkjær*, Botten is a good high-latitude station: bleak to a degree. The snow was close to the house, but within all one could wish: preserved meat, reindeer flesh, port wine, but no white bread; looms, spinning-wheels, snow shoes; many old ale bowls, saddles, carved boxes; and, at one end of the barn, boughs of trees brought up from the *dal* for the magpies to build in; at the other end a bunch of wheat, also brought up and placed on a pole for the birds. After leaving Botten we started for Haukelid Sæter, and found the men working on a new road to the Hardanger. As they progress, large monoliths are put up at intervals with the date of construction, and sometimes the elevation above the sea; here it is 2,800 feet, and at this point very large Scotch firs are found in skeleton state, monuments of a past period of giants.

HARDANGER.

HARDANGER.

HE Haukelid Sæter is 3,500 feet above the sea. Here we had the pleasure of meeting the Norwegian engineer of the road, and in the *vand* below were floating masses of ice. In the morning the *vand* was frozen (July 15), so that we could not cross in a boat, but had to go round. Near this was the scene of a reindeer slaughter by natives; they had a Remington breech-loading rifle; drove a herd into a *botten*, or *cul-de-sac*, and shot forty in six days—nine in one day; but we shall refer to this later on. On our journey we found the bridge carried away, and had to ford, which was great fun. We sent a knowing old pony over first. How we enjoyed it—one might have taken us for schoolboys out for a holiday—in and out of the water! One poor pony, however, did not find it agree with him, the ice-water was so cold, and for a time he was very bad indeed.

Once more in the flat of the valley, it seemed like old times, and we thought a hearty meal at Seljestad would do us good. In the latter respect, however, we were doomed to disappointment, meeting with nothing but picturesqueness and some costume, in which red bodices were conspicuous; so we had to fall back on potted meats and biscuits. Whilst waiting we saw some peasants *en route* for their *sæter*, with all their milk apparatus. The only good thing we got was a pony—a beauty

—to go down this grand valley, and drive, one may say, through the
Laathe Fos. At this point there are three falls in view of each other—
Laathe Fos, Espeland Fos, and Hildal Fos. This we enjoyed, and late
at night, or rather early in the morning—for it was one o'clock when
we got into the boat to go down the Sanden Vand and row to Odde—
having had such a good day, we sang "God save the Queen"
and many songs about Rensdyr, Jagt, Norwegian love, "det kjære
Hjem," &c.

In the morning we arose, and before breakfast read the following

Seljestad.

encouraging entry in the Dagbog :—"Wel Satisfed everything is good
order ; " and so we found it.

Rohdal itself is very beautiful. Our guide (Knut) returned to Haukelid,
and next morning we left the lensmand's house for a very long day,
hoping, if possible, to reach Odde. At Horæ we could only obtain some
sour milk, and then started over the snow for Seljestad, when we noticed
an old *bonde* preparing barley for brewing, assisted by his wife, with a
scarlet body to her jacket. About two P.M. we saw a grand effect of

Wooden Bridge at Roldal.

double solar rainbow—blue sky, no cloud. The sky between the inner
and outer circles, which were complete, was deep lavender. This was
seen from the head of the pass, above 3,500 feet, with snow all round us.
As we came down we cut our road, and after lunch, on arriving at the
outburst of snow-water, we were all wild enough to bathe in it.
However, we were none the worse, but, on the contrary, much the better
for it. Soon after we came on one of the grandest bursts in Norway;
a deep zigzag went down below us; and we looked upon the Gröndal,
which is immense, and at the end of which lies the vast expanse of the
Folgefond. We now began our descent, and worked along the valley.
The curious part of the fording was this—that the old pony, having taken
one man and baggage over, came back by himself, so that the "aspirants"
might swim over without any load. After this we had a long ascent
and heavy drag, beneath a scorching sun, over the snow, so much of
which had not been known for years, to a tiny Ligaret *sæter*. The best
thing to counteract the sun's influence is a sou'-wester hind side before.

"Rein" were seen here. Later on, at an altitude of 4,000 feet
on a bare rock, we partook of dinner, icing our claret *au naturel* in the
snow. Soon afterwards we began our descent, and, on leaving the snow,
found a young girl goatherd with a little bit of costume, showing that
she belonged to Roldal—viz. a dark blue cloth cap, with yellow-orange
border. Then we passed a hunters' hole or hut, and again forded;
finally coming, late in the evening, to a spot particularly mentioned by
Forrester and greatly admired by us—the old bridge, with torrent
roaring beneath, and the distant lake at our feet. We all paused, lay
down, and murmured with delight over the beauties of the spot. Now
that we had arrived at vegetation, we put leaves inside our caps, and
longed for glycerine for our faces.

Norway is grand, picturesque, wild, and bold, its principal features
being the long arms of the sea running inland for many miles, sea-water
dashing against the most precipitous façades of rocks, and the snow-water,
in many instances, coming down from the high ranges, and falling straight
into the sea itself. These arms of the sea are called *fjords*, and two
are especially grand and of immense expanse—the Sogne fjord (the

larger) and the Hardanger: both of them are rich in snow-scapes and
waterfalls. The Hardanger is the richer of the two in the matter of
waterfalls, having two to boast of—the Vöring Fos and the Skjæggedal
Fos, sometimes called the Ringedal Fos, as falling into the Ringedal
Vand. The Vöring Fos, which is approached from Vik, is better known

Odde: Hardanger.

than the latter, which is more grand in form and power: to reach it
one should stop at the end of the fjord. The difficulty of access and
roughness of road have prevented many from making the attempt; still
it is well worth any passing discomfort or fatigue to have the privilege
of communing with nature under such a combination of circumstances.

Arrived at Odde, arrangements must be made to remain at least three or four days, so as to visit the following most interesting localities:—

1. Skjæggedal Fos.
2. Buerbræ Glacier.
3. Folgefond.
4. Gröndal Laathe Fos, and other fosses.

The immense extent of the snow-fields of the Folgefond should not be missed, and for these a day not too bright should be specially selected: for pleasant as fine cloudless weather undoubtedly is, still nature is not always seen to the greatest advantage in it, and more particularly in mountain scenery, where mist and broken cloud relieve the various peaks, detach them one from the other by the most delicate films, and impart grandeur, endless variety, and size, draping the peaks with mystery and majesty. What a delightful sensation is that of rising on a fine fresh morning, with the early mist waiting its bidding to rise, and the anticipation of a glorious excursion in a mountainous country before one! Now for the fos.

The village of Odde, our starting-place, with its simple church, a station for carrioles and boats, its few wooden houses, kind simple people, and one lazy-looking sailing craft, or *jagt*, is fortunate in having a young guide, who, following in the steps of his father, has by his many good qualities influenced numerous people to visit this most excellent place; and all who have been there once seem to wish to go again. Our arrival from the Haukelid route, coming down the Gröndal, was late; in fact, about two A.M. Leaving the lake above Odde, we first caught sight of the Hardanger fjord, with the village lying below, the church in strong relief, and its few buildings against the bright water. One felt greatly inclined to sit and muse over such a scene, so calm, so peaceful, so solemn, so silent, for no singing birds ever chirrup in this northern land, and their absence is most noticeable.

Early in the morning we are up, and, with every promise of fine weather and comfort from our "nosebags" (most necessary items for this travelling), we start for the Skjæggedal, an excursion which should take fourteen hours to do comfortably. What enjoyment can there be,

what satisfaction, what knowledge gained in a strange country, if one
flies through it as if in training for some event or actually engaged in
athletic sports? The start is made from Odde down the lake to
Tyssedal, about an hour's row on the fjord. Soon is seen a white line
running out from the shore, the boat is caught by the stream and swung
round, and we near the land in the backwater. This is the exit of the
snow-water from the fos into the sea-water of the fjord.

Now to begin three hours' good steady walking up, up, up through
pine woods, with boot soles polished by slippery needles, now and then

Odde: Hardanger.

ledges of rocks, and ofttimes a shelving sweep of smooth rocks, dangerous
for most people, ticklish for every one, especially should they have any
tendency to giddiness. In some parts logs have been laid in the fissures,
and in one place a kind of all-fours ladder; still all enjoy it, and glory
in the freshness of the trip. After this tough walk the upper valley is
reached, and the farm, "Skjæggedal Gaard," is in sight. Here we
found milk and coffee; the homestead, so lonely in winter, now bright in
summer light, with peasant farm folk quite out of the world, and a
singing guide; but even Danjel, with his eagle profile, is not always

Skjæggedal Fos.

inclined to sing his best. Perhaps he is aware of the report that the priest, having heard that Danjel had fallen in love, had forbidden the banns, simply on the score of his too strong resemblance to the feathery tribe just mentioned.

Leaving the farm, we go down to the boathouse, covered with huge slabs of stone to prevent it being blown away by the wintry winds, and enter the boat to cross the river at the foot of the fos from the Ringedal Vand. Once over, we are soon at the Ringedal Lake, which is all snow-water, most crystally clear, and containing no fish, no life, on account of its extremely low temperature. On the left of the lake is seen high up the Tyssestrængene Fos, as shown under the initial letter of our opening chapter. Near the foot of this we stop to go up and see the bear self-shooter, or trap, where Bruin, it is hoped, may run against a wire which fires two barrels heavily charged—a bad look-out in the future for tourists who eschew guides, as this is the only accessible road. At the back is the immense snow expanse of the Folgefond, and in front of us we hear a distant roaring thud of continuous waters—our "fall." Rounding a point, we look up and see it. The best time is when the snow-water is in full spate; then it is truly majestic. The whole air seems whirled round in eddies; the water comes shooting and leaping over, falling in inverted rocket forms, half breaking on a ledge of rocks; the foam, the roar, the vast spray, everything is soaked and dripping — the energy of nature in a most sublime form, the Skjæggedal Fos itself. We were loath to leave the spot, but started off a little taciturn from the impression the scene had made on us, and safely returned to receive the kind hospitality of our friends at Odde, and next to visit the Buerbræ Glacier.

This glacier has especial interest for all lovers of nature, from the fact of its being not only a new formation or creation, but being still in process of development. It is caused by the immense pressure of the large snow-fields above in the Folgefond, which bodily weigh and force down the ice into the valley. Our good friend Tollefson, father of the young guide previously mentioned, was born in the valley where the glacier is now gradually carrying all before it. Fifty years ago, he told me, there were no symptoms of ice; gradually it formed and advanced—in 1870, ninety yards; in 1871, four yards in one week; and in 1874 a still more rapid progress. When we were there the front ice was just ploughing up a large rock and pushing it over; on either side the rocks are steep; and throughout the colour of the ice is very beautiful, rivalling the hues of the Rosenlain Grindelwald. Where will this glacier end? Most likely it will drive steadily on to the lake above Odde. Who can tell?

At the farm was seen a beautiful piece of carving, in the form of a

Buerbræ Glacier.

salt-box, very old, but well worth preserving. We shall give some specimens of native work further on.

The costume of this district is very striking and characteristic, the chief feature being the head-dress, or cap, called in Norske skaut. It is formed of white muslin crimped, the hair hidden by the white band over the forehead, the cap rising in a semicircle above the head, while the corners fall down the back in a point nearly to the waist; white linen sleeves, with scarlet body bound with black velvet; the stomacher worked in different coloured beads and bugles; the chemisette fastened with old silver brooches; and the collar joined either by a stud or brooch. The apron is equally picturesque. Like the cap, it is of white muslin, with three rows of open insertion-work on a pink ground, which is generally well thrown up by a dark petticoat, so that the whole costume produces a very striking effect.

These costumes were pleasingly brought together one evening when

The Spring Dance: Hardanger.

we were invited by Svend Tollefson to a little dance at his mother's house. The father and mother sat together, whilst the younger folk were either standing or sitting round. The fiddler was grand both in action and eccentricity, with tremendous catgut fire, a few involuntary notes trespassing now and then, and producing a stirring effect on the dancers. The young Svend, evidently a favourite with the youth and beauty of Odde, was continuous in his dancing, principally the Spring Dance—a waltz in which it is most desirable that the swain should be taller than the maiden, for the former, holding her hand over her head, has to run round the latter as she waltzes. The Halling Dance, in which the performer jumps a great height into the air, was attempted out of doors, but hardly with success. After each dance the guests partook of wine, and on this occasion we had some *gammel fiin kvid portvin* (fine old white port wine). The politeness of the Norwegians is most noticeable. After taking wine there was a constant shaking of hands, while the host was profusely thanked by, "Tak for vün," or "Tak for mad," the charm of which is considerably enhanced by the fact that these simple-hearted people mean what they say.

BERGEN AND ARCHÆOLOGY.

BERGEN AND ARCHÆOLOGY.

FROM ODDE DOWN SÖR FJORD—UTNE—HARDANGER FJORD—FAIRY TROLDS—BJERG TROLDS—THE HULDRE—THE NÖKKEN—THE NISSER—HAUGE FOLKET—TUFTI FOLKET—THE DRANGEN—CRACA, THE WITCH OF NORWAY—OLAF KYRKE, THE NORSE KING—BERGEN—THE HANSEATIC LEAGUE—THE GERMAN MERCHANTS—THE "PFEFFER JUNKERS"—THE FISH FOLK OF BERGEN—THE MUSEUM—STRAX—THE SILDE KONGE—NORWEGIAN WHALE SKELETONS—THE FLINT PERIOD—BRONZE PERIOD—INHUMATION AND CINERATION—ROMAN INFLUENCE—THE IRON PERIOD—ARCHÆOLOGICAL PERIODS IN NORWAY.

DDE is situated at the most southern point of the Sör fjord —the last inland effort of the Hardanger: and we left it with regret, although we knew there was a new world before us in sea-coast experiences; the most bracing sea air, together with the excitement of putting into all kinds of out-of-the-way villages nestling behind headlands and huge bastions of gneiss, to protect them from the furious gales which lash this coast from the south-west. We therefore laid ourselves out for thorough enjoyment of steamboat travelling, aided all down the Hardanger by the clearest and most lovely weather. We proceeded down the Sör fjord, *en route* to Eide, the boats coming off to the steamer at Utne. Some of the costumes were most brilliant in colour. One bright green bodice, the edging of which was blended with other colours, bore the palm, and everything bespoke joy save the face of the poor girl who wore it. She had come to see a brother start for America, and to wish him "God speed." Then away we went from Eide down the Hardanger to Rosendal, under the Folgefond. We had looked forward to visiting Rosendal, as the last château of Norway. Unfortunately there was not sufficient time to land. Sometimes, late in the season, the steamers visit outlying spots for cargo, and then

much may be seen, as, for instance, when the Bergen steamer calls at the
sulphur mines of Varalsoe.   On one of these occasions we not only had the
opportunity of going up to the mines, but through them, as five hundred
tons of ore were being shipped for England.   Some people find the steamer
journey wearying : there is, however, so much information to be gathered

The Market : Bergen.

from those who come on board, generally for short distances, that the local
details are always worth inquiring into.

The whole of the Hardanger is grand and impressive, the Folgefond,
with its immensity of snow-spread, being the chief attraction.   The peace
of fine weather makes one almost incredulous of what it is when winter
storms tear up the fjord, and the now unrippled surface is lashed into a
fury which defies the stoutest hearts and boats.

We are nearing Bergen, and there is a flutter on board as the town first opens to view—*mirabile dictu*, without rain. On the port side is a fort, and apparently there are fortifications on the starboard bow too. At last we enter the town.

NORWEGIAN FAIRY AND SPIRIT LORE.

Before travelling farther we shall do well to prepare ourselves for any

Rosendal.

unexpected apparitions, should such be our good fortune. Let us then review their varieties, as we hear them described by some who believe they have seen them. They may be classified as follows:—

The *Trold*, or *Eventyr Trold*—*eventyr* meaning "fairy tale"—is more frequently introduced into fairy tales than met by tourists, or even sportsmen; it is very shy of foreigners. This particular class is distinguished by having one, two, or three eyes, and sometimes one, three, six, or nine heads—a sort of giant, wild man, or inland Caliban of eighteen feet high.

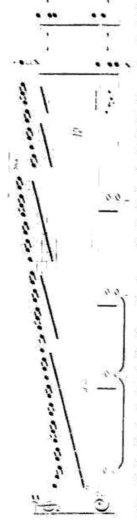

The *Bjerg Trold*, as the name suggests, frequents the mountains, and belongs to the same class as the former, though smaller, attaining a height of only twelve feet; in fact, it is a medium male ogre.

The Huldre.—This is a great fairy-tale mystery—the refined beauty in peasant Hardanger costume, who sometimes appears—as mentioned in our notes on Thelemarken—at dances and festivities, turning the heads of all the beaux of the evening until, in some swing of the spring dance, her dread cow-tail is revealed, when she vanishes as the music of D. T. A. Tellefsen suggests, leaving many broken hearts behind her.

Nøkken.—Water sprites, generally depicted with Neptune crowns, grey beards, and seaweed garments.

Nisser.—These are the mischievous little rascals who are always up to tricks here, there, and everywhere, and are closely allied to the sprites known in the Romsdal fjelds as the Höboken. These latter are seriously spoken of as existing, and having blue heads; and while up at the *sæters* a spare place inside is invariably left for them by the *piger.* The Nisser are depicted with grey clothes, long beards, short bodies, and red caps; the shortness of the body recalling to our minds a remark of days gone by, "Perhaps Mr. Nobody did it."

Hauge folket are a combination of Huldre and Nisser.

Tufti folket are a peculiar variety of Nisser.

Draugen are the ghosts or spirits of drowned persons.

Having classified these mystic folk, we can only hope that the information we have culled from authentic and local sources will not only help those who have already read Norwegian legends, but give a zest to those that may be forthcoming in future translations. Those interested in early witches will find details of Craca, the witch of Norway, in Olaus Magnus, "De Gentibus Septentrionalibus," a work probably well known to our immortal bard Shakspere, as Craca was great in using "venomous moisture of snakes." A caldron, too, was the common instrument of witches, wherein they boiled juices, herbs, worms, and entrails for enchantments.

Norwegian fairy tales are numerous, and traces of Trold lore are found all through the provinces, and constantly referred to in every-day life; at least, so we found. It is, however, possible that "the wish was father to the thought," and that we rather courted than avoided referring to them. Unfortunately they came not, although a rattle of flying rocks down a *couloir* was always attributed to them. We shall not find them in Bergen, that is certain; only Huldre appears in public, and she coyly at the festivities: she delights not in war-paint, *gibuses*, or opera hats.

Olaf Kyrre, the old Norse king, built, or rather developed, Bergen into a town about 1070. Easy of access, and naturally adapted as a centre for trade, it has now become the most important commercial town of the west coast. The principal tradition of Bergen is, that ever since the introduction of umbrellas every little Bergenite has been presented with one as soon as born, another being bestowed by the godfathers and godmothers at confirmation; and it is only reasonable to suppose that at a wedding every one gives the bride a Sangster or a Gamp, according to circumstances. Anyhow, it is an indisputable fact that umbrellas are plentiful in Bergen, and, when not devoted to keeping off the rain, they serve as a screen against the occasional visits of the sun. No doubt this humidity is owing to the position of the town, which lies between two mountains not less than 2,500 feet high, upon and around which Jupiter Pluvius reigns supreme.

Passing from the climate, we must notice the town or city. Approaching it from the fjord, it looks picturesque and busy, with merchantmen, steam tugs, steam launches, and coasting steamers entering the harbour. On the left is the old castle or palace, with the remains of its banqueting hall, supposed to have been built by Olaf at the same time as the church. On the right is the landing-place for steamers, above which, on a part of the town abutting on the fjord and forming a continuation of the principal street, is a fort. Proceeding farther down the harbour, with the churches before us, on the left we pass the ship-building yard, and come upon a long line of white wooden houses with wharfs in front of them—a busy scene, fraught with energy and *bouquet de stokfiske.* Alongside lie the Nordland *jægts,* or vessels which bring the fish down dried from the Lofoden Islands, and their crews are in close commercial relationship with the owners of the white wooden structures which are known by the name of the Hanseatic Houses. Olaf Kyrre had favoured the Scotch with certain privileges for trading at Bergen, but in after years the Hanseatic League made great efforts in the same direction, and successfully; for in 1228 they settled and began to trade in Bergen, and by some extraordinary means ousted the Scotch and English entirely by 1312, when they were left in their trading glory. They soon developed the vast fishing trade of Nordland, and made Bergen the great commercial centre which it now is, receiving dried cod-fish and roes from the north. These are sent, in exchange for wine, corn, iron, and so forth, to Sweden, Denmark, Holland, Spain, England, and various parts of the Mediterranean, but especially to the Roman Catholic countries. Still, these German merchants were not entirely happy; they, the Hanseatics, located together on one side of the harbour, were not much liked by the youth and beauty of the Bergen proper side of the town, receiving from the Norske *piger,* or Bergen beauties, the characteristic and appropriate *sobriquet* of "Pepper Youngsters" (*Pfeffer Junkers*), which still clings to them.

Bergen must have been very imposing in appearance in the old times, when the large Hanseatic craft were warping out of the entrance of the

Bazen.

harbour, with their high quarter-deck and taffrail-deck lamps, squarely rigged three masts and steeving bowsprit, jack-yard and water-sail, long pennons and streamers from the yard-arms, the sides of the vessel falling well in, and the guns bristling to frighten any who might take a fancy to the good cargo on board. Now the Hanseatic League is a matter of ancient history, but it did its work well, and will not soon be forgotten. Bergen is at present the source of supply to all places to the north of it, and in itself is interesting to the visitor as being a centre of costume—that charming relic of days almost bygone, when each district had its distinctive dress and its special form of silver ornament, which, however quaint, or, to go further, even ugly, still commanded favour by the respect its presence offered to those who had gone before, and most likely had worn it. The costumes are well seen at the market, when the farmers, or *bønder*, come in with farm produce, bringing their wives and daughters, with the milk in wooden kegs formed like churns, with leather stretched over the top, and hoops pressed down tightly to keep it from spilling. These milk-cans are carried by the women on their backs, with straps or ropes, like knapsacks. One costume is very noticeable here, that of the fish-girls. It consists of a dark blue petticoat and jacket, a kind of Scotch bonnet well pulled over the head, with a white edging of cap coming a little down and showing all round, and roll upon roll of kerchief round their necks. Robust, pictures of health, and muscular, how they row! When their husbands or brothers are with them they row all the same, being quite capable of the first law of nature—self-preservation. They work hard and in earnest, and always look *bien soignés*. For flow of language the early fish market conveys a good idea of the activity of the tongue and power of gesticulation—features of life not common to Norway. The boats are all down below, and the purchasers, generally domestic servants, hang over the woodwork above, craning their necks and stretching down, pointing first to this, and then to that, and possibly pushed aside ere long by some one else worming in for a bargain.

In the meantime the fishermen in the boats are taking it very quietly, sorting their fish, feeling that their purchasers can be supplied *strax*.

Now this word in the dictionary is described thus:—" *Strax*, directly or immediately." Practically, in Norwegian life, the traveller finds that it is no such thing, *strax* being a movable feast—so movable that it is impossible to say where it will be. It is not even so sure as the "Coming, sir," mumbled by a flying waiter in the midst of a crowd of customers about one o'clock; for in the latter case, if you wait until two o'clock, you feel there is a probability looming, but with a Norwegian *strax*, especially if applied to getting horses for carrioles, it may be hours, or, in the words of what was thought a charming song in our younger days, though now half forgotten, " It may be for years, or it may be for ever."

Bergen is especially associated with the registers of the sea serpent; therefore the subject should be referred to here. Crews and captains have voluntarily sworn to having seen in various parts of the ocean strange monsters of the deep, usually of serpentine form; and judging from the illustrations in that interesting work by Olaus Magnus the Goth, "De Gentibus Septentrionalibus" (dated A.D. 1530), the sea monsters depicted therein were enough to frighten any artist, particularly if he were on the spot where the said creatures were visible. Still many wonders of the deep may be studied with advantage at the Bergen Museum. Lately this institution has been brought prominently to light, thanks to the energy of M. Lorange, who has found a grand field for his enthusiasm in Scandinavian relics, flint implements, and specimens of the "glorious Viking period." But we must not be carried away by this interesting topic from paying due attention to a strange-looking creature in this museum, which is kept in spirits and labelled—

" SILDE KONGE (*Gymnetrus Glesne Ascanius*).

"Length (dried), without tail, 12 feet. Depth, 1 foot. Head blunt, square. Bristles, or capillaries, 3 feet; 8 from above, 6 under the chin."

The whales are very fine and enormous specimens, being eighty feet long. Why, then, should there not be gigantic *silder?* A Highlander was once speaking of the grandeur and size of Scotland, when a remark was made that the area was small. "Tout, tout, mon! But if you saw it rolled out, just think what it would be then!" So, were we to roll out a

Bergen: Fish Market in the distance.

ninety-foot whale, should we not have as good a sea serpent as any newspaper might desire?

Now that costume is being fast swept away, the old silver of Norway bought up by travelling dealers for the town silversmiths to export, the old carving replaced by cheap feather-edge boarding, and the *mangel brats* chased away by "Baker's patent" or some other brand-new patent, a general national museum like this of Bergen becomes especially desirable, and even necessary, for retaining in the country itself its own characteristics. In flint weapons it is especially rich, thanks to M. Lorange, who has opened many tumuli with reverence and care, his perfect knowledge of the subject being a guarantee that nothing will be overlooked. Natural history, too, is well represented. The corals found at the entrances to the fjords are astonishing, immense, being more like shrubs in size. The Runic inscriptions and carvings, portals, and chairs are most interesting; while the church decorations of early Christian periods, the ironwork, arms, and numismatic records, so useful as collateral history and in the assignment or corroboration of the dates of tumuli, are well cared for. Most heartily, therefore, do we wish success to the national collection now so happily commenced, and so full of promise.

The somewhat modern appearance of Bergen and the absence of old wooden houses are attributable to the disastrous fires which have raged from time to time in different parts of the city; in fact, so much was destroyed by the great fire in 1702, that nearly the whole of the town has been rebuilt, except the old Hanseatic houses. Neither has Bergen escaped its share of scourges, for the black pestilence made sad havoc about 1348 or 1350, and the plague destroyed immense numbers about 1620.

Although Bergen is the most important fish mart in Norway, it will be better to give a detailed description of its working, extent, and season, when we arrive at the Lofoden fishing grounds and islands, and the coast of Heligoland and Salten. It seems curious that these slow-sailing *jægts* should come five hundred miles with their cargo of fish, when Trondhjem, Molde, and Aalesund are close to hand; but on consideration it will be easily understood what an advantage it must be for them to get a quick and ready sale for their fish, and a selection of every kind of produce from the warmer climates of the Mediterranean, or even the West Indies. Whether articles of necessity or luxury, Bergen can supply anything, from a marlinespike to a sea serpent.

The museum of antiquities at Bergen now deserves attention, and in it the Nordfjord is brought especially before us, as we shall see hereafter. In the meantime we will turn to a few chronological landmarks in the early days of Gamle Norge, which will be most valuable, as the catena of Scandinavian history is complete in specimens of the different periods, corroborated by the archæological treasures of Denmark, now so admirably

Church Candlestand : Bergen Museum.

arranged by Professor Worsaae in the museum at Copenhagen, and the collection of antiquities at Stockholm. Having followed out these different periods, we need only casually refer to the objects themselves when we come to the districts where they were originally discovered or still exist.

The Flint Period.—For a long time it was supposed that Norway had no stone period : now flint implements of beautiful surface and exquisite finish are found up to lat. 65 , beyond which, and near the North Cape, the implements are of hard schist, the local formation of that part. Among these specimens are found of arrow and spear heads, and knives. The hammers are generally made of whatever the rock of the country may be. This use of hard schist for stone implements is corroborated by discoveries in similar latitudes in Sweden and Finland. A very fine dolmen is still in existence at Frederickshald, in the south of Norway—a spot which, to judge from the number of tumuli in the neighbourhood, generally placed on rising ground within view of the sea, is a perfect cemetery. Their average height is about 3 feet 6 inches to 4 feet, and length about 35 feet. Near Stavanger the flint implements are of exquisite finish.

The Bronze Period.—It is interesting to associate this period with two systems of burial, namely, Inhumation and Cineration.

Inhumation.—Wooden coffin—a tree scooped out; at the bottom was

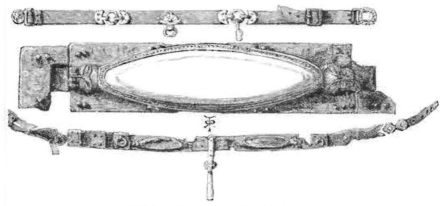

Knife-stone on Bronze Belt: Bergen Museum.

placed a bullock's skin, on which the hero was laid in his garments, and with his arms by his side. An instance occurred in which the following items were preserved quite perfectly:—A *vadmel;* a kind of Phrygian cap: a wool plaid and petticoat, or rather kilt, to the knee; a small box; a comb; and a bronze sword and knife. These, with a belt for the waist, convey a vivid idea of the costume of the period.

Cineration.—Flint stones seem to have been the base of the grave, which was about seven feet long. Remains of cinders prove that the skin of some animal was first laid down, then the body with extra garments, in the cinders of which the bones were found, accompanied by a bronze sword, with sheath ; two knives of bronze ; and a cube of wood, not burnt. The bronze implements are so generally known that it is not necessary to illustrate them.

The Iron Period.—During this period the tumuli were consumed on elevated positions within view of the sea ; the bones discovered are burnt, the ashes being in urns. The objects burnt with them were generally small ornaments of bronze or iron, the workmanship of which betrays no Roman influence. Sometimes, also, glass vessels were consumed, as globules of melted glass have been occasionally found. In other cases the ashes are in bronze vases, showing a transition state. Should there, however, be any swords, they are bent and twisted, and are undoubtedly attributable to Roman influence, as some of the bronze vases bear Roman

Hard Schist Implements: North Cape.

inscriptions. The next stage covered a large space, and was characterized sometimes by cineration, and sometimes by inhumation. In the latter case the objects are placed with great care after the old Roman manner, and consist of urns of burnt clay, bronze, and glass ; ornaments, arms, &c. Here we have not only actual Roman work, but Norwegian imitations, such as bracteates, which have been found with Byzantine moneys struck about A.D. 450 or 500. This brings us to an important epoch in Scandinavian history, which is very ably described by Dexter Hawkins, Esq., in a pamphlet on the Anglo-Saxon Race, being an address read by him before the Syracuse University, June 21, 1875 :—

"THE ANGLO-SAXON RACE.

" A providential event, not originating from themselves, but from a Roman emperor who intended no such results, occurred at the close of the third century, which, by directing the attention of the Saxons to maritime exploits on a larger scale, with greater prospects, and to more distant countries than before, exerted an important influence upon their own destiny and that of Europe, and finally of America.

"The Emperor Probus, harassed by the annual incursions of the bar-

Sword : Bergen Museum.

barous hordes around the Euxine, now the Black Sea, transplanted a large body of various tribes, including Saxons from the vicinity of the Elbe, to that region to serve as a protection against future inroads. But the attachment of mankind to the scenes of their childhood, and their ardent longing

Bracelet : Bergen Museum.

when in foreign lands for the country their relatives inhabit, where their most pleasing associations have been formed, where their individual characters have been acquired, and customs like to their own exist, are feelings so natural to every bosom, and so common to every age, that it is

Rowlock Knot of Birch-tiwes.   Viking Rowlock.

not surprising that these exiles longed to return to their native wilds. Impelled by this desire, they seized the earliest opportunity of abandoning their foreign settlements and possessing themselves of the ships lying in

the adjacent harbours; they formed the daring plan of sailing back to the
Rhine, though they were more than two thousand miles distant by sea, with
no charts, compass, or pilots, and ignorant of the many islands, and shoals,
and currents of the Black and Mediterranean Seas. Compelled to land
wherever they could for supplies, safety, and information, they ravaged the
coasts of Asia and Greece. Arriving at Sicily, they attacked and plundered

Sword Handle: Bergen Museum.

its capital with great slaughter. Beaten about by the winds, often ignorant
where they were, seeking subsistence, pillaging to obtain it, and excited to
new plunder by the successful depredations they had already committed,
they carried their hostilities to several districts of Africa. They were
driven off that continent by a force sent for that purpose from Carthage.
Turning towards Europe, they passed the pillars of Hercules, sailed out
into the Atlantic Ocean, rounded the Iberian peninsula, crossed the stormy

Bay of Biscay, passed through the British Channel, and finally terminated their remarkable voyage by reaching their fatherland at the mouth of the Elbe.

"This wonderful expedition discovered to these adventurers and to their neighbours, to all, in short, who heard, and had the courage to imitate, that from the Roman colonies a rich harvest of spoil might be gathered if sought for by sea. It removed the veil of terror that hung over distant

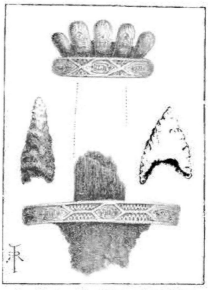

Arrow Heads and Sword Handle : Bergen Museum.

oceans and foreign expeditions; for these exiles had desolated every province almost with impunity. They had plunder to exhibit sufficient to fire the avarice of every spectator. They had acquired skill which those who joined them might soon inherit. On land the Roman tactics and discipline were generally invincible; but at sea they were comparatively unskilled and weak. The Saxons perceived this, and immediately turned their whole attention to naval warfare. Like their American descendants, they were cunning and apt at whatever they undertook. Their navy became so effective in a few years that every country in Europe bordering on the sea had contributed to their wealth, and they annoyed the Roman commerce to such a degree that large fleets were fitted out against them, and an officer appointed by the Romans as early as the beginning of the fifth century styled 'The Superintendent of the Saxon Shore.' These exploits had filled their island with wealth."

A very interesting antiquarian discovery was made in 1877 close to a village in Sealand, some twenty miles from Copenhagen, of which the following are the most important details:—About three yards below the ground a grave was discovered, surrounded and covered by large monoliths, the grave being about six yards long and two yards wide, and the floor consisting of rough oaken planks, on which were found the remains of a female in a mummified state. Round the head of the body were placed several glass cups, one of which bore an inscription, in Greek characters, signifying "Good luck to you," and in other cups were found the remains of various kinds of fish, as well as a gold coin of the reign of the Roman Emperor Probus. A solid ring of gold encircled the neck, and a heavy pin of the same metal was also found close to the body, as well as a couple of finger rings. At the feet were placed several vessels hollowed out of oak, in which were deposited the bones of various animals, especially young pigs, and in one of these basins were discovered forty-two dice burned in bone. In the earth round this tomb were discovered the remains of several human beings lying in great disorder, and it is supposed that the bones are those of slaves sacrificed to the manes of the deceased lady. It is thought probable that this tomb dates as far back as the third or fourth century after Christ.

With regard to the initial letter at the head of this chapter, it is from a remarkable specimen of Runic wood-carving—part of an old episcopal seat—which will be more fully described when considering that class of work, of which we find such interesting specimens in the museums of Norway, especially that of Bergen, and which happily are well preserved for our study and guidance.

ARCHÆOLOGICAL PERIODS OF NORWAY.

A.D.	STONE.—Silex for stone implements.—Arctic stone implements recently discovered near the North Cape are of hard schist, the stone found in that part.		
100 200	BRONZE.—Period of Cineration and Inhumation in wood, trees scooped out.		
300 400 500	IRON, 1ST PERIOD.—Sudden transition from cast bronze swords to iron swords damascened. —Roman coins found in tumuli of 63 A.D.— 217 A.D.—Iron and glass come together.— Roman influence.	Urns for ashes.	
560 600 700	IRON, 2ND PERIOD. Byzantine Barbaric influence.	Byzantine Coins. Roman Bracteates.	
800 900 1030	IRON, 3RD PERIOD. VIKING PERIOD. Christianity. RUNIC 1ST PERIOD.	Norsemen to Iceland.	**A.D.** 863 Harold Harfager. 936 Haco the Good. 994 Olaf. 1000 Eric and Sweyn.

WEST COAST AND NORDFJORD.

WEST COAST AND NORDFJORD.

RAVELLING in Norway is principally carried on by carriole, row boat, and steamer. From the immense extent of seaboard the latter mode has naturally been much practised and developed, more especially as the Government has not only countenanced it, but encouraged it in every possible way. Our route in this excursion involves the adoption of this mode of conveyance, and we leave Bergen, with all its interesting monuments, associations, costumes, and commercial interests, to wend our way up the coast to the north. Starting from the port, with its varieties of shipping from all parts of Europe, its Nordlander *jægts* always prominent, its churches standing well out from the moist haze and smoke of the city, a scene at all times picturesque, we soon settle down for steamboat travelling. On this occasion there was a very unusual bustle at the mouth of the port, a fresh breeze was blowing, and a small schooner yacht was being towed out for a trial trip. From the amount of bunting and excitement, not only on board the yacht, but on shore and on our steamer, this was

L

evidently a great event. With sails all ready to be hoisted as soon as the
hawser was let go, one would imagine that chase was about to be given
to a smuggler, or that a Viking had appeared in the offing. It was, however, only for a sail, and our little coast steamer was soon away by herself,
ploughing in loneliness through the fjord. And now for the healthy
pleasant delights of sea-coast trips.

With our luggage quietly stowed awaiting our bidding, and a calm
satisfaction that the steamer was well found, our meals punctual and
plenteous, our captain well up to his work, the steward anxious to take
care of us, and our travelling companions likely to be agreeable—the
Norwegians being kindly to strangers who are courteous to them—there
is but one drawback to the steamer work. It occurs in the fore part of
the vessel, and is occasioned thus. A *skaal* (health) for Gamle Norge is
a very good thing and a noble sentiment, but if too often repeated, with
the usual accompaniments, it becomes offensive. The peasants come on
board at the numerous stations, and can procure every variety of spirit
which is unobtainable on shore. They therefore make the most of their
opportunity, and soon the demon of our own land—inebriation—appears,
bringing discomfort to the recipient, disgust and misery to his surroundings, and finally a besotted and wrecked old age; for, although strong
constitutions may resist its inroads for a time, they must inevitably
succumb at last, and pay the penalty. Either the victim is quarrelsome
or maudlingly stupid; the demon makes his mark in so many ways.
The natural expression of the features is no more to be found; the eye
loses its brightness, its sweetness is changed for heavy moistness, its tele-
graphic and sensitive expression has vanished; the lips, before so full of
character, are no longer the exponents of subtle feeling; the hand
trembles, the feet shuffle, the whole frame is limp, the muscles are flaccid,
and the brain muddled to futile dreaming. If this be a curse in public,
what must it be when it invades a home! Well may the wife long to see
her husband freed from this evil spirit and restored to his former noble
nature!

But let us turn to the feast to which nature invites us. At every
moment the sea-scape changes, new peaks open to us, the clouds are

The Village and Church of Alva.

massing ready to be gilded by the setting sun, and soon we have the heavens in a blaze of fiery glory and impressive grandeur. As we approach the outlying islands we find strong glacial markings, less vegetation, and the characteristics of the line of route, all up the west coast of Norway, can be carefully and comfortably studied by the most moderate sailors, as the islands keep the steamer track quite smooth, and it is only when the entrance of some large fjord is passed that any motion is felt or any rolling occurs. The villages generally nestle close to the waterside, the church in the centre, and the *prestgaard* close by; but a variation occurs in one village particularly: the church answers the double purpose of God's service and the fisher's beacon, and is placed well upon the top of the hill. Many are the excuses made by professing Christians for not going to church, but the difficulty of access to the one in question, while frequently causing the pilgrim to utter the cry of "Excelsior," at the same time elicits the mental avowal that he would be very thankful if it were lower.

In making this passage those who are in Norway for the first time must be struck by seeing that both sides of the vessel are sometimes within three feet of the bare rocks, which descend precipitously into the sea. No wonder, then, that the old woodcuts of the sixteenth century show large rings in the face of sea rocks for the vessels to moor to.[*] One part of the coast near Steensund is most barren: the masses of rock, entirely rounded by ice in past ages, seem to be too smooth for vegetation to get a footing. The spot, however, finds favour with lobsters, which seem to thrive here, ultimately finding themselves in England, and ending their days with a garnishing of parsley. Even for lobsters, however, travelling is very expensive, for the difference between their price in England and Norway is simply astonishing.

On some parts of the west coast red deer are found, and now that these animals are scarce, it seems a pity they should be in danger of extermination. Better far would it be if the *chasseur* had sufficient strength of mind and self-denial to induce him to give these last of their race such a respite, or series of closed seasons, as would enable them to increase in

Vide Olaus Magnus.

number. One fine head came on board—a very healthy, powerful horn, and royal on both sides. The beam was much thicker than it usually is in the horns of stags killed in Scotland, and very grand in form. The haunch weighed thirty-eight pounds English, so that it must have been a "gude beastie."

After passing the entrance of the Sogne fjord and experiencing a little rolling, we sighted the island of Alden, a very imposing mass of rock, supposed to resemble a lion's head; and, fortunately for us, there

Ousen.

was less mist rolling around it than usual. It would have been a sad disappointment had we only had its whereabouts suggested to us, which is the fate of many who are anxious to see it. Our wholesome little craft soon leaves Alden far behind, running up Dalsfjord to the eastward; we begin to worm our way through narrow passages, with the rocks nearer than ever to her sides; and at last we leave her to take a boat, in order that we may row up to Ousen, a lovely spot, with such garden roofs and such a farmhouse and buildings! The spot where we landed is shown in the woodcut. The river was of the most beautiful soda-water-bottle colour, the wooden buildings topped with the mountain ash in all its gala beauty of bright clusters of berries. The beams used in the construction of the houses were very old and remarkably massive,

and the size of the Sea House suggests the importance of this locality as a centre for general merchandise. We arrived here about three in the morning, and the servant at the farmhouse showed us to our rooms, which had a weird ghostly appearance from their bareness, size, and height. The old staircase testified that it had once been well kept up; and then, as we looked about for some indication of date, we at last found a good specimen of a snaphance pistol of about 1625, which tallied well with the period we had already assigned to the house. We had now left the sea for a time, and after a few hours' rest the Tentmaster - general reported everything ready for a start; and soon we were *en route* for Sande.

The Island of Alden.

Sande is a place of sweet waters to the traveller. After rough roads, bad beds, sparse food, and occasional parasites, what a change! The probability is that a stranger would pass the comfortable-looking house, with its creepers over the porch, its well-stocked garden, English home life, and generally inviting appearance. The geniality and kindly welcome offered by the master of the house are most delightful, and every one who visits it has a strong wish to rest for awhile in such agreeable quarters. The valley is very bold and grand, and good expeditions can be made in all directions. The Paymaster-general, with honest pride, pointed out to us where, on a former visit, he had killed a fine fish, and seemed to

Nordfjord Peasants.

realise the fact that, having once experienced that gratification, you can go on killing the same fish, with all its pleasant associations, for the rest of your life. But we soon had to leave this inviting spot for rougher quarters, being bound due north, to be up for August 1st and reindeer; and as time, tide, and August 1st wait for no man, we started for our next station—Nedre Vasenden, on the Jolster Vand.

On arriving there no luxuriant garden growth welcomed us. Instead of a south aspect, it was a north one. The atmosphere was changed, and we missed our beloved Sande. As it was Saturday night, we looked forward to a quiet Sunday, with church, the meeting of the peasants, and a good chance of seeing all the costumes of the district, which is wild, barren, and uncultivated. The Sunday morning was inviting, and we took the opportunity of going to the lake, at a retired spot where the mountain path came down to the water's edge, for a quiet bathe; but no sooner were we in the water than a troop of peasant girls came slowly down the path. Confusion and dismay! Norwegians do not understand our amphibious tendencies. However, No. 1, with his characteristic retiring disposition, dived, leaving a certain disturbance of the water after his plunge, which attracted attention. Beyond this, only the smallest possible part of two heads might be seen. Now came the anxiety of wondering what the spectators would do. Would they throw stones at us, to make us run, or examine the contents of the chief's pockets, or try on some of our garments? No; while wishing we had the epidermis of a Captain Webb the whole group suddenly laughed, and moved slowly off, evidently thinking how curious the English were in their habits. We afterwards met at the church porch.

EVERY traveller taking to pony travelling in Norway implicitly believes that there is no danger of the animal ever falling; and it is a happy and comfortable faith. The *blakken* are rare good animals, cream-coloured, with dark points; hog manes like hat-brushes, with white down the centre, the black being outside; and their hind legs rather zebra marked. From the first they are petted, and their intelligence and stolid kindliness requite the care of the owners. They trot well; and how they can go down a hill! As they crouch and run close to the ground they need never be handed: no "'ands" required, as the British groom would describe it. Still, exception proves the rule, and we met with an instance in this *stolkjær* trip.

We were going over the crest of a grand mountain road, below us

a large lake, and beyond a glorious range of mountains.   The deep tone
of the fir forest added solemnity to the scene, and our good health and
enjoyment of such company made it a happy moment.   The Paymaster-
general was leading—driving fast, as was his wont; for his driving was
like the driving of Jehu.   The Tentmaster-general was next, with a huge
Norwegian sitting by his side.   In a second came the transformation
scene—nothing visible to the Patriarchal eye but the soles of the boots
of the two persons in the *stolkjœr*, the expanse of the huge Norwegian
foot forming a contrast to the small neat extremity of the Tentmaster, who
was shot out with great velocity, and stunned by his unavoidable concus-
sion with the earth.   We laid him in the heather by the side of the
road, anxious for his recovery.   Happily he soon came round, but was

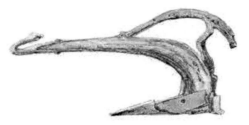

Norwegian Plough.

much shaken; it was, therefore, necessary to proceed very gently to avoid
further shaking, and we purposed halting for a day or two, until we could
get the advice of a doctor.   It assumes the form of real travel when
doctors are two days distant or more, and you carry your own lint and
medicine.   Thankful were we to see the return of the old smile on the
Tentmaster's face, and to hear from his own lips the welcome bulletin,
"I am better."   The pony was not hurt, while the big Norwegian had
a *dutt* of whiskey, and, we fancied, was ready to be thrown out again to
obtain a second remedy.   Soon afterwards we arrived at Jolster Vand by
Nedre Vasenden.

The station here is a huge—may we say dreary?—wooden house.   The
next morning, however, brought its joys and happy combination of circum-

The Friendly Toilette.

stances: the invalid was much better, the bright July morning perfect; there was service at the annex kirk along the *vand*, or lake; and we purposed going by boat with some peasants, and a most enjoyable row it was. As we neared the church we found many boats already arrived, and, invited by the loveliness of the morning, the beauties of Jolster had congregated and were looking their best. Many *stolkjers* were standing round the walls of the churchyard, and the ponies were enjoying themselves, nibbling the short grass as far round as their tether would allow them. There were some quaint costumes. These good church-going peasantry arrive early; and, as many dwell so far apart, and seldom meet except on these occasions or on some special business, we cannot be surprised to find that, instead of opening the meeting with prayer, the practice on the part of the men is to indulge in a little worldly talk before church, while the girls, according to custom, complete their toilettes from the contents of their *tines*, or travelling boxes, the said contents being a mixture of old silver brooches, silk handkerchiefs, and *fladbrod*: in some cases the butter is carried separately in a small *tine*. One incident struck us very forcibly—the kindly interest the girls took in the neatness and finish of each other's dress. Only fancy three nice-looking *piger*, or girls, sitting one behind the other, each plaiting the hair of the girl in front of her. What absence of mystery as to capillary arrangements! No "Lady Audley's Secret" (which *Punch* said was her back hair). No; each girl wished her friend to look her best, and carefully adjusted a string here or a brooch elsewhere, for there were no looking-glasses about. Then there were several other objects of interest. The black caps of the Jolster women are very curious, with a little white showing all round the edge. The covering up or hiding of the hair has a very mediæval appearance, but the nice little stand-up collars give a more modern character to the neck. The plaiting of their homespun dresses is very close indeed.

On this occasion there were two or three knots of people, suggestive of something of unusual interest; and we found the centre of each to be a little baby brought to be christened, surrounded by admiring relatives. Such babies! such funny little chrysalis-looking pets, swaddled and rolled up! the swaddling-bands being of many colours, the more brilliant the better—red, white, green, and crimson—with the cross frequently introduced, and generally so worked as to come uppermost in the band. The swaddling process seems much the same as in Brittany, where a ring is sometimes fastened at the back by which to hang the child up while the mother goes to work. No one could have seen this peaceful Sunday morning

The Lych Gate, Nordfjord.

without being struck with the beautifully clean appearance of every one there—the homespun (*vadmel*) looked so sound, and so likely to wear well; the old silver ornaments so respectable and heirloomy. Of course on week-days, when the women are seen in the roughest of their outdoor life, it would be unreasonable to expect to find them as neat and prim as on Sunday. What a contrast, too, did this glorious sunshine and

Sauce, looking down the Valley.

joyous meeting present to the bleak dark days of winter, when perhaps a hundred and fifty pairs of snow shoes, eight feet long, are set up round the church, waiting their owners' bidding to start *home !*

After this cheerful interlude we went on to the next station—if such it could be called. We intended making a meal there, and rather looked forward to it; but nothing, not a single thing, could be had. We therefore made a fire, and into a black pot put some portable soup, with slices of Brand's gravy-looking biscuits. Whilst the Tentmaster tried to do the soup the Patriarch in vain sought a wooden spoon; not even that was to be got; so the soup was stirred and tasted with a birch twig. But he made a discovery: whilst spoon-hunting in a drawer, which would only partly open, he saw the end of a mutton bone; perseverance was rewarded, the drawer was opened; but the result worse than a blank, for the shoulder-blade bone of mutton was bare, save the green fluffy mould in which it was mantled. Some people may say, "Not so bad; soup and biscuit, biscuit and soup, is a change." Still, in long journeys with *stolkjars* over rough ground, you can form no idea how shaky and restless it becomes. Moral: always carry a spoon, and, above all things, never start anywhere without a nosebag with plenty in it.

This Nordfjord district is one of special interest now, as recent dis-coveries have corroborated the old traditions of its close association with the Viking period—a period bearing so powerfully on our own national character, that the subject should be fully investigated, and the extant remains of the Sea Kings' real life placed carefully before us. For the nonce it will suffice to refer to one particular tumulus, recently dis-covered and opened in Nordfjord. As Denmark rejoices in, and is much indebted to, the archæological enthusiasm, deep research, and sound knowledge of Professor Worsaae, so Norway is fortunate in having the devotion of M. Lorange, who not only tries to lay these precious earth-bound relics before us, but actually rescues them for our benefit and that of posterity; not only interests the dry antiquarian and connoisseur, but in a far larger way draws more closely together the bonds of union and interest between nations. It is remarkable that a Roman emperor was the means of developing the sea powers of the Scandinavians rather than they themselves; for only recently some interesting coins of Marcus Aurelius have been found in a tumulus in Denmark.

The contents of the Nordfjord tumulus were as follows:—Boat with iron rivets twenty-five mètres long; a bit; fifty-four bosses of shields, or umbos; stirrup; a drinking bowl of immense interest, and well enamelled; sword, with silver work; key of treasure chest, spear head, bone comb inlaid with colour, gold ring, dice, arrows, deck marbles, beads and amulets, bones of horse and kid, belt of bronze, and belt-knife.

Having heard what tradition says about the funeral rites of the great ones, the contents of this tumulus, as well as the numismatic discoveries in Denmark, are especially interesting, as corroborative of history. We are much indebted to pagan customs and rites for the valuable materials brought to light in connection with this period. With Odin for their Mars, or god of war, and Thor for their god of air and storm, they believed that their mighty men and heroes would pass to Walhalla, and there enjoy the future in the same way, but more perfectly, that they enjoyed themselves here upon earth—strong symptoms of their belief in the resurrection of the body. For this purpose they buried with the defunct all his implements of war and chase; the horse was killed and placed in readiness, and, should he be pleased to row, his boat was there too. In the Nordfjord case the bowl is especially fine. Notice the delicate work in the base of it; in the woodcut the upper subject is the bottom of the bowl. The enamel is very minute; the "chequer" design, one might say, very Scotch. The enamel is only on the base of the bowl; the body is of bronze, and the upper rim is ornamented by three heads, one of which is shown in the centre of the illustration. This is drawn full size, and the base of the bowl one quarter size.

The two buttons are of single wire, very rudely but cleverly arranged, with shanks not likely to be pulled away from the body. These are of gold.

The key of the treasure chest would suggest that many good things had been stored therein. Still the list is so complete that we could hardly expect more items than those recorded.

Bronze Bowl, with Enamel Case, Swords of Viking Period: Bergen Museum.

The ivory or bone comb is a fine specimen, and the coloured work well preserved.

The dice also are rather curious, as being a little longer than quite square.

One of the most remarkable features, however, in the contents of this tumulus is a set of bone marbles about one inch in diameter. The sphere or marble is flat at the bottom, and has a small hole in it. These marbles were used by men who spent their lives in ships, and were played with on deck, the flat base being intended to keep them steady, while the holes at the bottom, fitting on to small pegs in the deck or board, prevented them from sliding as the vessel lurched. There was a most interesting discussion on this matter at the Society of Arts. Deck marbles were a novelty. Professor Bryce suggested that deck draughts would be a solution of the difficulty; and after referring to the antiquity of the game of draughts and the modes of playing, Professor Maguierson gave a dissertation on the ancient game of " merelles," known in Iceland and Scandinavia as " mylla ;" and even in the present day the shepherds and boys on our South Downs cut the same pattern in the close turf, and play the same game. We therefore come to the conclusion that these bone treasures had been used on board the vessels of the mighty Sea Kings of old, the little pegs, as just observed, preventing their slipping, and also the hero from losing his temper and using " pure Saxon." The same precaution is in these days applied to railway chessmen, and also those intended for use on shipboard, each figure having its peg for safety and security. " Nothing new under the sun," said the wise man, and true is it.

Eleven o'clock at night, four thousand feet above the sea, we find ourselves at the top of the pass, just above Udvig, looking over Nordfjord. After a long day, and a very hard one, pleasantly tired, we enjoy the scene before us : peace and tranquillity, with snow poles all along to suggest what winter made it. The happy moment has arrived to commence the descent. " Half the pleasure is in the anticipation," has often been remarked : we all thought this about half-way down this precipitous descent in the twilight. The torrent path seemed filled with boulders, the ponies slid, the bipeds stumbled, and by the time we were half-way down we had no knees left. This is one of the roughest ascents and descents in Norway, and is hardly practicable for any kind of carriage: still it is one of the things to be done, and one of the charms of the country. Lazy people lose much of the grand scenery with which it abounds. Steady going tells best, and those who try to spurt early in the day are much the worse for it afterwards. How steadily an old Swiss guide starts off, and keeps at his pace, on and on! That is the only way to last. By this time we see a flickering light down below: we long for

The Pass; Holdestadt.

it, and soon arrive, but very late—about one o'clock A.M. We knock at the door of the station, which is really a private house, like that at Aurjhem, but selected by the Government to facilitate the wanderings of travellers. We are therefore the more indebted for the kind welcome we receive. Down comes the young son Jules, who immediately recognises our Tentmaster-general. Soon we have some refreshment; and not long afterwards Master Jules says, "Jeg schal go seng" ("I shall go to bed"). So said all of us—and we went.

In the morning we were up early. A bathe in the fjord was our first thought, although the big stones are much against it, and the seaweed spoils it: the only way is to take a header out of the boat. After

The Post arriving at Uskvig.

breakfast we espied a novelty in water travel: a large birch bough was seen approaching, which we soon discerned to be the postman availing himself of a fair wind after the usual custom here, a sail being too dangerous even with sheet in hand. The original and simple practice of cutting a large birch bough, and putting it in the bow of the boat, serves the purpose better, the fresh foliage holding the light air, and helping very materially the rower, who is frequently, as in the present case, of the gentler sex, but very strong. The postman sits complacently in the stern of the boat, with his bugle just announcing his arrival, and rousing up the inhabitants of the quiet village of Udvig. The bag is not large, but most important in appearance—a huge leathern mass, locked, barred, and bolted. The boat speedily comes to land, and the well-known sound and scrape are heard. The bag is soon out, and the postman also: the post has arrived at Udvig.

Postman and his Carriage.

We rowed out on the fjord to look up at the pass we had come down so early in the morning; the view was very grand, backed by the higher ranges of the Justedal snow. We had next to visit one spot which seemed a great favourite with the host and hostess, and therefore started off, and soon reached a position, having followed a strong stream or burn which came above a saw-mill, looking over which the whole fjord lay at our feet, the mountains on the other side looming stupendously.

Returning, we visited the church and lych gate (see p. 82), the latter narrower and higher than usual. When we regained our station a new phase of life awaited and burst upon us. An invitation to a dance! It was somebody's birthday—the nineteenth—a young visitor from Stockholm. Would we join in the festivities? We were delighted to have the opportunity of visiting a family on such an occasion; but the dancing element alarmed us when we thought of our rough boots and our walk down, we being rather particular, and knowing what boots should be. What was to be done? We shall see.

In the meantime two boats were watched with much interest: one

The Saw-Mill. Udvig.

contained the domine and family, the other some well-to-do friends. The hearty welcome they received was beautiful; their sweet simplicity and genuine affection were charming, and certainly will never be forgotten by us, their visitors. Soon after the arrival the repast or dinner was announced, and the real Norwegian customs were well placed before us.

After one course the master and lady of the house waited on us, every guest getting a knife and fork; and at the end of each we went and shook hands with the host and hostess, the children kissing their parents.* After the fish and various solids we adjourned to another room for fruit, *patisserie*, coffee, and, not an unwise thing in Norway, a cigar. The next event was to adjourn to the garden to see a glorious sunset over the fjord,

Falendet: Nordfjord.

and to finish the cigar. During this agreeable part of the evening the youthful Jules, with his nice fair face, came and asked if the "English gentlemen would come and play with the girls in the garden." The Patriarch of our party sent his two young bachelor companions, who

* This has been referred to in former books, we are well aware, but could we omit a custom so expressive of gratitude? *Le bon Dieu donne tout;* but do we always give thanks?

readily accepted the invitation with a spontaneous "Oh jag!" Report says the amusements in the garden were a combination of hide-and-seek, Tom Tiddler's ground, and prisoner's base. Anyhow they all seemed to have enjoyed them; in fact, the Patriarch often regretted afterwards he did not join the youthful throng instead of remaining with the seniors. Still there was much festivity in store, and the Patriarch took kindly to the dance, which included schottisches, mazourkas, and valses. This brings us to the boot question. The dance commenced. The evening began merrily. The piano (for there was a piano, and a good one, from Christiania) was in tune, and all were thoroughly enjoying themselves, when

The Olden River.

attention was drawn to one dancer in particular. Sage as an owl, how silently this youthful Achilles glided! How softly yet firmly he trod the polished boards, for no juniper tips were scattered that evening on the floor! Why was it? The Paymaster-general, equal to the occasion, was dancing in goloshes! O shades of Scandinavian gods! O Thor and Odin! that this should be the result of civilisation in Kjære Gamle Norge!

Another great feature in the evening was the singing and the national music—and how we did enjoy it! Need we say how they sang, and we tried to sing, "The Hardanger," by H. Kjerulf, and the chorus song of "Norsk Sjømandssang," by Grieg, which goes with such grand emphasis; and the light tripping sweetness of "Ingrids Vise," also by Kjerulf, with its chorus of "Over Lynget, over Lynget?" * Another, specially bright and cheery, touched the Patriarch very deeply: he is often heard still humming this air "without words," which the merry dancer described as being all about some beautiful creature with large blue eyes and golden hair. If she had but been with us to have danced with the goloshes, what would she have thought?

* See page 14.

It was a delightful opportunity for us to see the *vie intime* of a nice family in Norway. The welcome was most cordial; and thankful were we to find ourselves unexpectedly in a spot which every one tried to make us feel to be our home. Long may Herr Hammer, Madame Hammer, and their kindly family enjoy health and prosperity! and, might we say, continue their kindness and attention to those who go to Udvig?—for it seems a perfect pleasure to them to do so.

There was a disinclination to hurry from Udvig in spite of the fine trip before us, for it is a lovely row up the Nordfjord. The Tentmaster-general seemed loath to leave, he was so pleased with Jules; he thought he had grown—had so improved; and he determined on several good openings for him in London. The Paymaster-general had evidently made a great impression, and no wonder, with the happy combination of youth, a petite, petted dark moustache, and enthusiastic forehead and goloshes, to say nothing of really good firework execution on the

Lyth Fishing.

Christiania piano. We were horrified afterwards to find that all this had induced the young ladies to ask him to write all our names on a pane of glass. In a weak moment he yielded; but why did he? How often have complaints been made by ourselves of the creatures who carved and wrote names! There were, perhaps, extenuating circumstances in this case. So farewell to Udvig and its pleasant associations.

And now for a start up the Nordfjord to Faleidet. Such a good boat was supplied by Herr Hammer! How we enjoyed it, looking forward to our drive from Faleidet! We soon came upon a number of boats fishing for *lyth*, a fish caught in large numbers, easily taken, readily consumed; there were a great many boats, and they fish with a deep-sea single line, feeling the bite over the forefinger, as in Scotland. We wanted much to have seen some of the red sea-fish taken, which are much larger than

the mullet, but redder in tone and of splendid colour: a noble fish to look
at when caught, but poor on table.

Falcidet is a good station, beautifully clean, and well situated over the
water. Here we were much interested in specimens of copper ore, on the
richness of which our native held forth most fluently. The ore was decidedly
good, and I think in his own mind the Tentmaster had promoted a company,
and probably thought of the youthful Jules as assistant secretary and foreign
correspondent. No time was to be lost, so we hastened to our *stolkjærs*, but
hardly had we reached the top of the hill when the Patriarch's gimlet eye
saw a long birch horn near a shed by the roadside. This could not be
resisted. " Halt ! " was the word, whilst the others went on. They soon
pulled up, for the too-tooing was noisy, if deficient in harmony; still
there was a certain satisfaction in the fact that one had elicited sound
from a long birch horn, as used by the good people of Falcidet, inferior as
these horns are in force to steam fog-horns, as now used at the
Foreland, or the steamboat whistle which skewers the tympanum of every
traveller at every stopping place, be it where it may. There is a great
charm in all these old-fashioned ways of doing things. Again the girls
call to their cows, singing to them in very sweet strains, and the cows follow
them. It is no question of a subtle tin-tack looking them up, which, like
the county of Buckingham, runs into Oxon and Herts. The whole treatment
of animals in Norway is a good example: the kindness is consistent and
the care unceasing. The early training of the children has much to do
with this: at all events the youthful impressions and the influence of the
parents have never lost one iota of good.

The Nordfjord is a great inlet of the sea which runs up an immense
distance, and greatly favoured the Viking tendencies. Many fine remains
have been discovered, and the contents of one tumulus in particular, now
carefully preserved in the museum at Bergen, have been already laid
before the reader.

LEAVING the Nordfjord and passing through much that is grand, we start from Faleidet, and when we arrive at Haugen have a glorious view of the Horningdals Vand. Our hopes are buoyant, for it is a "fast" station; and our appetites are good. What natural beauty around us! To be happy, however, requires a combination that is seldom realised. In this case one thing was wanting, and to travellers such as ourselves it was a most important item—namely, food. The station was fair to view. On the stone steps young children were playing; and the numerous family were nursing each other—rollicking, chubby-faced, and unwashed: for Norwegian children they were merry. In the road in front of the house was standing a gaunt figure in knee-breeches and stockings; and, with his braces hauling on to the short waist, his long hair, and his straggling beard, he made a good type of what he really was—a slayer of bears. Above the entrance, over the merry group of children, were two bears' skulls—the triumph, joy, and pride of the slayer. Being short of provisions, we soon went on a voyage of discovery, and investigated the interior; but what a blank it proved! The fast station folk knew nothing, or pretended to know nothing. "A cradle" of good carved wood, a bed in the corner of the room, and a fireplace seemed to be all in this homestead. The only *fladbröd* we could procure was of that unwelcome class prepared for travelling, which means that it is flabby and tough enough to be rolled up and folded without breaking. When the practical reader thinks of the shaking, jolting, convulsive jerking action of *stolkjærs*, and even carrioles, no wonder this food is left rather doughy for its journey. Happy the man who, when he meets with this material, can set it up on end! Dry it to the oat-cake condition, then it is good indeed—very good. Still we made the best of it, and came to the conclusion that one of the charms of travel is the variety of situation: and then, after all, with pleasant companions, anything short of bad accidents is only the kind of thing which the true traveller must expect, and almost seeks. So we looked

forward to the next good meal we could get, but which must be very late
in the day.

Some one suggested the advisability of smoking down our appetites.
That was declined as injudicious, and we longed to reach Hellesylt. The
second stage on, near Haugen, we saw a wonderful peak. Some
idea of its towering grandeur may be formed by setting its printed name

Haugen, near Hellesylt.

on end. It has no end of a name: here it is—Horningdalskrakken.
What a pity one cannot have time to "do" all these peaks, this one
especially, isolated as it is, and commanding a most interesting range,
with so many fjords at its feet, and the Hjørrendfjord and its shriven
peaks bristling below! In these days of express trains, fish torpedoes going
twenty knots an hour, telegrams, and instantaneous photographs, people

will not give sufficient time to do anything with steady enjoyment. Skurry and scuttle are too prominent by far.

As we approach Hellesylt the mountains become higher, more bluff, their formation more tortuous, and we anxiously begin to look out for our descent to the station—town one cannot call it; in fact, hardly a village. Arrived at the top of the pass, with the river dashing and splashing, the

The Horningdalskrakken, near Haugen.

zigzag of the road is like patent cucumber scissors—twenty zigzags or more. At one's feet lie the Storfjord, the Geiranger district, and Søndmur. Of course there is the usual church, most prominently posted, with a good station, to welcome those who escape from Haugen's natural grandeur to the stomachic comfort of Hellesylt. What a good meal we all thought supper was that night! It was not the mere pleasure of going in for a meal, but we had felt the want of it, and now were thankful to enjoy thoroughly the good cheer before us. There are very few parts of Norway which exceed the grandeur of the neighbourhood of this place. The Storfjord is immensely grand, but the Geiranger is a climax. The steamer from Hellesylt to Aalesund goes down the Storfjord, affording a great variety of scenery, with considerable comfort to passengers, as the vessels are well served; and in this case the steamer has a captain known to all who have travelled here, and always remembered with the most pleasing associations. Captain Dahl has done much for this district, and has opened up the unparalleled Geiranger fjord. Are not his good qualities recognised and noticed throughout Norway by ladies? Having said so much, we hope to visit Geiranger again under the captain's kind care.

At Hellesylt we all noticed a prevalence of brass-mounted belts among the men. Norwegian belts have invaded England and taken it by storm, from the luxurious productions of a Thornhill, regardless of price, to the other extreme, the Birmingham wholesale harum-scarum article, which loses its gloss in a few hours. The Norwegian belt is a national characteristic, adopted by both sexes, being worn on all occasions and for various purposes. An instance occurred when two were used during a trip to keep on a linseed poultice; but this was a modern innovation.

We were up early indeed the morning after arrival at Hellesylt. What a morning! Hardly a breath as the steamer lay at the little pier waiting for us. We had arranged with Captain Dahl to go up the Geiranger as far as Maraak, so as to pass the glorious fall of the " Seven Sisters," and see it in all its beauty. We were very fortunate in all the circumstances connected with this visit—weather fine, scenery grand, cicerone full of enthusiasm and information, companions reliable, food, after Haugen, one may say " good, plentiful and good." The characteristic features of this Geiranger, which has only been known to travellers during the last few years, are the extremely precipitous façade of rocks that enclose it, the paucity of landing places, and its beautiful fall, the Seven Sisters. We arrived at the foot of it about six o'clock A.M., and, as the sun was well to the eastward, the effect was fairylike—the prismatic

Hildsøyli.

rays seemed to pervade the base of the fall. The Seven Sisters come over and take their first flight some two thousand feet above the fjord, and the streams, seven in number, according to the pressure of melted snow above, combine and separate, lose themselves in spray and spoondrift, and then collect again from the dripping face of the rock, and finally the whole base is "gauzed," so to speak, with the dash of mist and the prismatic rays called by sailors "blossoms"—really portions of rainbows. We wanted to linger over the beauty of this spot—such delicacy of form, as the streams shot forth some of the rocket jets, losing themselves for a time, and then collecting with renewed energy for the final dash into the fjord; but at last even Captain Dahl goes ahead, and we steam on for Maraak, at the end of the fjord. Opposite to the falls we see a relic of old Scandinavian paganism. Jutting from steep rocks, of two thousand or three thousand feet, above a solitary boathouse, is shown a prominent rock, called the "Pulpit," and above that the gigantic profile of a Viking; while higher still are situated some farms, well away from modern improvements.

A Breenstok, or Bucket for Sharpening Stone.

If any one dies there during the winter the inhabitants keep the body until the snow is sufficiently melted to allow of its being brought down for conveyance to Hellesylt. It is their custom also to tether their children, for the "go-cart" conveyance of the seventeenth century, as shown in Quarles's "Emblems," would soon be over the edge, urging its wild career to the depths below. The very thought of such a position would be enough to frighten some people; but how happy in themselves are these poor folks in their simple belief and faith, their home love and trust! How difficult is it to consider this kind of happiness, when the same family goes on in the same position in life for three or four hundred years, in the same costume, and with the same old silver ornaments! "How bad for trade!" some would say. "What stagnation! how slow!" Yet how enviable when we have tasted the bitters of overstrained brain-work, and the furious competition of millions of people, all massed and arrayed for the daily struggle of modern times! It is from this latter that men retire for awhile to take a refresher, a change of air and circumstance becoming a matter of necessity; and so London, after a season of gaiety and rush, is left in favour of outlandish places, simple fare, and, in fact, to get away from the daily jostle of life, to be ready for the next bout.

After our return from Maraak, Captain Dahl continued his passage towards Aalesund. The Geiranger features were less marked until we arrived at an immense perpendicular surface of rock, evidently but recently exposed to view; and its appearance is explained by the fact that some years ago the whole facing of this mountain came bodily down into the fjord, raising an immense wave which swept across the expanse of water, and almost entirely destroyed the village on the opposite side. A more recent case occurred in the Nordfjord. The Hornelen Mountain rises majestically from the fjord, going down from Bryggen. Out of compliment to this monarch and giant a new steamer was named after it; and, on the first occasion of passing, the captain honoured Hornelen with a salvo, which was promptly answered by a great mass of rock being launched from the mountain side, throwing up a wave which nearly annihilated the saluters, and frightened some of them so much that they will never venture to repeat their *feu de joie*. It is equally dangerous to disturb or cause any considerable vibration in the atmosphere under glacial ice or snowdrift: many lives have been lost in this way, and the fact cannot be too strenuously impressed on the minds of all travellers.

The Geiranger Fjord : Seven Sisters Fall.

MOLDE AND ROMSDAL.

MOLDE AND ROMSDAL.

TO those going northward Molde has especial interest
for many reasons: its situation is beautiful, its
climate delightful, its vegetation luxuriant, its
flora abundant, and, as a centre to radiate from,
it is most convenient. To arrive there one
becomes associated *pro tem.* with the good ship
Tasso. "Good ship" is used, in this instance,
as a term of affection among old Norwegians.
In former days it was rarely that any save real sportsmen or regular
fishers were to be found on board. Every one was known. The steward
knew every one by name; the captain looked forward to seeing his
"regulars," and could tell exactly how much he would see of each individual
passenger. Judging from the weather, he could guess the number for each
festive meal in the saloon, and knew without a doubt who would propose to
smoke a cigar on deck, or one more pipe before turning in, and who would
be ready to spin a good yarn if there were any chance of conversation
flagging. From Hull to Trondhjem a fraternity existed, on condition
that no one betrayed undue curiosity about his fellow-traveller's river.
That condition carried out, any one might kill his fish over and over

again, and even add a pound or two, rather than the relater should not be happy. The captain of the *Tasso* was decidedly a favourite, and

The Landing-place: Molde.

could the weather at all times have proved as fair as the captain himself, the *Tasso* would have been always crowded with passengers; for even in spite of the stormy winds of the North Sea there has been such a thing as a telegram for the captain, hoping he would wait for the next train, as —— wanted to go by the *Tasso*. There is much sentiment about this dear old vessel. Light as a cork, in a breeze she can throw you up off your legs, and catch you somehow when you come down. She is lively, but that is better than being driven through everything, tunnelling the long seas. Besides, if the Saturday be very bad, and Saturday night too, Sunday afternoon generally improves matters, and by the evening some ladies venture up in the captain-cabin on deck for a little fresh air, and are well looked after; for the captain himself, in spite of having been up all night, comes out with his personal appearance unimpaired, and buttoning his gloves, which he wears only on Sundays. He had a very impressive way of buttoning the right glove, as if a great work had just been completed, and the mere act would revive the passengers. Still he was a thorough sailor and a great favourite, and everybody regrets that he no longer commands the *Tasso.*

This vessel, which leaves Hull on Friday night, with her course north-east, ploughs, or rather bruises, the North Sea until Monday morning, when the first land is made, which is generally Statland—bluff, wild, precipitous, and if not almost uninhabited, at all events very sparsely populated. Having made this point, the *Tasso*, altering her course, runs up the coast for Aalesund, before reaching which the number of passengers on deck increases. Passengers are always divided into two classes — the well and

Molde, from above the Town.

the unwell, or "marines." It is surprising how strongly the marines muster at this point, and discover that they would have come up before

if they had known there was anything really worth getting up for. Not a
syllable do they utter about how they envied those humble people who
were always asking for more roast beef, and who relished bottled stout.
Neptune's habit of rocking stops many a hearty meal, and keeps many a
visitor from Norway, levelling even the great and mighty; for even
the president of a learned society has been seen lying on the deck,
rolled up in a blanket, with the large red letters "Scandinavia" across

Sea Warehouse : Molde.

his vertebræ, helpless and mute, though his object in coming was to talk
Norske; but the sea god denied him the luxury until he arrived at the
land of Thor and Odin. Aalesund will be described afterwards.

The *Tasso* arrives at Molde on Monday afternoon or evening, according
to the run. If it is a fine evening, what a lovely sight after the
permanent unbroken horizon of the last three days! On the left lies
Molde; on the right, mountains, snow ranges, islands, and fjord entrances
running up to Veblungsnæs, Alfernæs, and Eikesdal. Some have described

Molde as a Naples; but the two places are as different as is Stockholm—sometimes called the Venice of the North—from Venice itself. Let each have praise for its individual beauty and grandeur, but no comparison can well be made.

The *Tasso* does not come alongside; the small coasting steamers do. Boats, therefore, come out, when one soon sees what seamen these Norse-

The Flower Market: Molde.

men are; and the women are as good as the men. The principal figure as well as the voice most distinctly heard is that of Jacob, the polyglot and ubiquitous porter from the hotel. Molde was once famous for an hotel kept by Herr Buck and family, whose kindly reception and unceasing attention were a pleasure to the visitor. In front of the house were honeysuckles, clustering roses, geraniums—not yet called pelargoniums at Molde—wallflowers, fuchsias, and almost every kind of flower. With such good quarters, such attention, and such natural beauty, how could any one be disappointed in Molde? Yet so it was; one's fancy was blighted by the footmark of civilisation—modern dress had supplanted costume. The *taille de Paris* was attempted, although it has not, up to this time, much reduced the general solidity of the Scandinavian waist. The heads of the people are much more transformed, and soon become smiling victims to the first phases of the vile taste for artificial flowers, feathers, and tawdry finery. If they only knew the dignity of simplicity and the charm of good

The Churchyard: Molde.

silver ornaments handed down for generations, they would never so debase themselves.

Molde is almost entirely built of wooden houses painted white. In the lower basement the storehouses run out over the water for some distance, being built on most picturesque piles of timber, with solid galleries, affording delightful peeps seaward. This warm spot, nestling under the mountains, faces the south, and is naturally celebrated for the vigour of its vegetation and the luxuriance of every variety of floral growth, which is centred in the churchyard, where every Moldean tries to outvie his neighbour in the culture of fair flowers on the graves of those dear ones who have been called home. What a beautiful thought is this to keep before one through life—to be called home, and to look upon death as a friend, or as a schoolboy does upon his exit! Happy indeed are those who can do so! It has a soothing influence, which conduces to cheerfulness in old age; and what is cheerfulness in old age but a looming of the immortality of the soul, as the outer case begins to fade away?

This lovely spot has been selected as the best locality for an establishment to solace the poor victims of that terrible scourge of the North—leprosy. White as a leper, and shining as Gehazi, Elijah's servant—that is the aspect of Eastern leprosy. Not so in the North. The features of the Northern leper become purple and hard, and the feet swollen and fearfully disfigured. It is brought on by the absence of vegetable diet and the constant use of salt fish. The hospital is situated outside the town, on the south-west side, and is coloured yellow.

Many routes start from Molde, and much character may be noticed on board the steamers—small practical craft, with very efficient captains—good seamen and remarkably obliging—a quality most acceptable to the traveller. But this attention is only accorded to those who adopt the axiom of the late Dr. Norman Macleod, who said the best language to travel with was, " Yes, if you please," and " No, I thank you," whether in domestic life or *en voyage*. It would conduce greatly to home harmony if this were more generally adopted. It is a wholesome contrast to a wood-cut in *Punch* by that keen observer of human nature, John Leech, who portrayed a Transatlantic brother holding a revolver at the head of the person sitting next to him, adding only the simple words, "Pass the mustard." To return, however, to the deck of the steamer.

The lower class in Norway chew and expectorate; the upper class smoke, and some carry pipes. Carry is the correct term, for the pipe belongs to the class impedimenta. As the map of France is divided into departments, so may be the travelling pipe of Norway. First department, the mouthpiece; next, the elastic, to ease off the roll of steamer or jostle of stranger; then a huge silver tassel, generally two; then a stem and a joint; and finally the bowl of meerschaum. What an *écume de mer*! What a responsibility to travel with such an instrument! It is quite an apparatus —worse than a *narghile* or *chibouque*; less coil, but more tassel. The bowl of the pipe is generally surmounted by a huge silver cover in the form of a crown. Our woodcut gives a specimen of one in the possession of an officer on a tour of inspection along the coast or fjord. As he is represented with his back to the land, it is only just to mention that there was some object of interest in front of him.

One more word for the *Tasso.* Returning from Trondhjem, she generally calls at Molde. Should bad weather come on, the waiting for twenty-four or forty-eight hours in constant expectation is wearying to a degree. One hardly dare patronise the good baths of Molde, admirably

The Coast Inspector.

arranged as they are, so unmercifully do the jelly-fish sting; but the advantages of sea-bathing are irresistible, so, in spite of being stung, we indulge in a bath while waiting for the steamer, and in the midst of it we hear the alarming whistle of the *Tasso.* Rapid exit and hurry-skurry, in which tradition says the Tentmaster-general, anxious to be first, was last, from having tried to put on his flannel shirt without towelling sufficiently beforehand. Hurried as we were, there was still a ceremony to go through, which could not be omitted without giving offence. The bath attendant is most careful in his attention to visitors, who generally give him twopence. On receiving this honorarium he observes an old custom in Norway, that of shaking hands and thanking the donor; so we all kept up the good old charter, and received his kind wishes for our safe return to England and our homes. Unquestionably we carried with us delightful recollections of the kindness of the people, and especially of the *bonder* folk—many souvenirs to remind us of localities visited, and very deep impressions of the charm of their simple life, undisturbed, as it seemed, by those little envyings, strivings, emulations, and jealousies which, like mosquitoes, sting and irritate, to the misery of their unhappy victims.

Veblungsnes: Romsdal.

Surely the man who loves God, worships Him through nature, and traces his majesty in creation, would enjoy the spot depicted in the woodcut, where the village of Veblungsnæs is shown close to the edge of the fjord, backed by the snow range. What a neighbourhood to have round one! And what a contrast to the idea conveyed by the same word in modern acceptation! Here the sea-water of the fjord washes the edges of the hamlet, in many parts bluffly repelled by huge and mighty façades of rocks; there a ravine terminates in a waterfall into the sea itself. Valleys branch off in all directions, excursions are numerous, and many new ones still remain unexplored. The high fjeld is easy of access from Veblungsnæs, and real bear valleys are near, where Bruin exists and has met with his death at the hands of our countrymen. Natives have offered to go on the terms of "no bear, no pay." This betokens an amount of practical confidence which is a prominent feature in all bargains between Scandinavians and our folk. Bruin is still a terror in some parts, and especially to the *sæter* people, or *piger*. For instance, near Isterdal the following circumstance occurred to a friend:—Scene, lonely *sæter*. English traveller approaching. *Pige* appears at window imploring help and beseeching traveller's assistance. A bear has been down, and killed a cow. The *pige* positively dare not come out until the Englishman shoots the bear that killed the cow that frightened the *pige*. Now comes the sad finale. The dead cow could not be found, neither could the bear; and even had the latter been discovered, the traveller had no rifle to shoot him with. Still there can be no doubt of there being many yet left to be laid low by our enthusiastic fellow-hunters in days to come. Veblungsnæs is hardly appreciated by travellers, who are generally so bent on rushing forward to the well-known comforts of Aak, that they are blind to the beauty *en route*. Perhaps an innate longing to get away from villages makes them anxious to dive at once to the more placid and less populated parts. This place is generally reached by those who come from Molde by steamer, in which case the entrance to the Romsdal fjord is a grand subject, affording the most magnificent mountain and sea-scape combined. Happier far is the traveller who goes in a small sailing boat, with a good south-wester behind him, a tight sheet, and the water hissing away all round her, thrown off from her bows and rushing from her stern, as the crew lie down singing good Norske songs, some of which are as long as Gaelic ones; and that is saying a good deal.

Veblungsnæs is close to the mouth of the Rauma, which rises in Lesje Vand, and after forcing its way through rocks and every kind of obstruction, finally finishes its course among peaceful sand plains. The village can boast of many good things. First, the church, or *kirke*, then the post-office, telegraph office, station for carrioles, a compulsory school, a baker of white bread, *præstegaard*, and a pier, to say nothing of the store or shop. Having made a bouquet of these charms, let us refer to them *seriatim.*

The church is the old wooden structure from Gryten which was buried in the sand, and stood, as shown by the spire on the right hand side of the illustration, looking from Næss. It was moved about fifty years ago, and at that time was painted red, having only of late years assumed the more sombre hue which now characterizes its roof and spire—namely, black. The interior is plain fir; the pulpit is high up over the altar, and of a general light blue tone; while on the right side, on the ground, is the bishop's stall, panelled up to the galleries, which go round the church. The candelabrum that hangs in the centre from the ceiling is very elegant in design, and made of pinchbeck; it is dated 1770. The silver candlesticks on the altar, one on each side, are large and massive; these are lighted three times a year—Christmas, Easter, and at the end of the forty days. The first priest appointed to Gryten commenced his work in 1514.

Here we saw a funeral, which was largely attended, as the church is on a main road. The coffin was followed by seven *stolkjærs* and many people, some of whom had driven on before; but there was no clergyman to officiate.

The post-office is kept in a very unofficial way. Calling one day, we found that the *post kontourress* (who, by the way, is a very superior person) was not at home, having left her official duties to assist at four o'clock tea—*soirée.* The postman is picturesque, with an enormous portmanteau, with irons, chains, and such fastenings, to assist in the protection of which he carries a horn and a revolver (see p. 87). He goes from this office to Dombaas, so that sometimes, from the difference of elevation, he will sledge one part regularly, and carriole the other. Before leaving the post-office we will thank the *chef* for all her kind attentions to us and many of our countrymen.

The telegraph office is admirable. English spoken, and every information.

The carriole station is at Herr Onsum's, who seems to be the squire of

Carriole crossing a River.

Veblungsnæs. Here *tout est Onsum*—hotel, boats, land, and store. Every one has a good word for the member of the Storthing, Herr Onsum, and his musical and well-educated family.

The school is, throughout Norway, for all denominations, and compulsory.

As to the baker of white bread, this personage is mentioned because white-bread bakers are few and far between, and a valuable adjunct to Fiva, where we stopped. Twice a week "our daughter" drove in from Fiva to the baker at Veblungsnæs, about nine miles in and nine out,

Sometimes the white bread was not ready, and after a nine-mile carriole drive, with a long ford across the river, it is rather trying to go back empty-handed. Occasionally there were additions, such as *rφd fiske*, or red sea-fish, like very large mullet, hanging from the carriole, and picturesque in colour, to say nothing of odd baskets banging about. We must some time have a sketch of "The Return from Market through the Ford, with the Skyd-gut Boy behind." Our daughter's boy was rather an old one, Ole Fiva as he called himself—the *gamel skyd-gut*. The occasional one was very

Næs.

young, and very nice indeed: as he did not understand English, his answers resolved themselves almost always into the "blushing grin" of good-hearted innocence. At last "mee boy Matthias"—pronounced *Mattæus*—found an outlet for his feelings, and brought red berries, or *tyttebær* in his cap; and when he found them accepted, and that his offering gave us pleasure, he grinned and blushed more than ever. But why were we not sure of getting our white bread when we sent so far for it, hail, rain, or shine? For this reason. One day there was a glorious breeze out in the fjord, the white horses were showing their crests, while the gulls and terns were sweeping round us. What a day for a sail! Herr Onsum had a good sea-boat, and would be sure to lend it to us if we asked. We did. My wife, daughter, self, Ole Fiva, with three Norwegians, full of sea-rovers' expeditions and sagas, for a crew, were soon on board. As the craft was lying by the landing-place her bowsprit naturally rose up and down as the waves heaved her hull, when a voice came from the end of it : "Ole, Ole! Spørge, Ole, spørge!" Ole took no notice, and again came the same appeal from a figure with a white cap and jacket. It was the baker of the white bread, hanging on with a desperate effort, asking permission to go for a sail with us instead of getting our *vid brød* ready for us to take back. Judging from the uncertain movements of the applicant, it is to be feared the supply of white bread is equally precarious at Veblungsnæs.

Our view of Næss is taken as looking up the Rauma River. On the left are the Vengetinderne, the Karlstrotind, and the Romsdal Horn over the valley, down which flows the river Rauma by Aak ; the centre peak is the Mid-dag Horn ; and on the right is the Isterdal valley, with the Biskop and Drönningen towering above. The little spire of Gryten is inserted here to show where it stood before its sand immersion and removal to its present resting-place. From this point one obtains a grand view and general idea of the immense sand and grit deposit collected here from the two valleys of the Rauma and Ister, the greater portion of which was ground off the sides of the valleys by the great glaciers when the glacial period was in full action, and before all the mighty ice giants melted at the presence of the new visitor to the coasts of Norway, the gulf stream. All down the valleys the rocks are worn and ground round by the *débris* in the ice as it passed down. Only some such phenomenon as that referred to could have so raised the temperature and worked such changes.

On the following page an old friend is shown at work by the river-side—Ole Larsen, a shoemaker of simple habits and small *clientèle*, but very large family, about eighteen in number. Unlike many of our followers of St. Crispin, he begins *ab initio*, with the skin as removed from the animal, and is now getting the hair off previously to tanning.

It can well be imagined that Ole Larsen does not do a large business in the course of the financial year, and the family seldom get meat, their whole nourishment being *bröd og smör*, bunkers, and cow comforts.

The Norwegian farm-building is called a *laave*, and is so constructed that the hay-carts can drive right in under cover, and be unladen at convenience; underneath are generally stables and a cow-house. Such a *laave* as the one shown on p. 116 will hold three ponies and about twelve cows. During the summer the cows all go up to the *sæter*, and about

Ole Larsen, our Shoemaker.

September return to the valleys, preparatory to their winter session, when, poor things, they are generally shut up from October right through the winter, till spring comes with all her brightness, and releases these long-pent prisoners from their thraldom. It is an amusing sight to see them first at liberty when the snow has melted in the valley. They gallop, kick, frisk, career, and chase each other; and the ponies join in the festivities with the cows and the goats, and rejoice together for a time, until all finally agree that there is nothing like good-quiet steady grazing, to which they betake themselves.

ERE seems centred all that is grand in nature, bold in outline, interesting in geological formation, with the constant registers of the ice passage down the valley, as it existed before the glacial period was melted away by the influence of the gulf stream. The whole valley suggests the idea of the crust of the earth having cracked in cooling, the fissures forming these immense valleys. At the entrance of the latter, as the river approaches the fjords or the sea, large plateaux of sand have been deposited in past ages, and through these sandhills the river forces its way, very frequently altering its course, until finally it reaches the sea. These sand plateaux or ridges are very distinctly shown at the entrance of the Rauma River, a little above Veblungsnæs, and being exposed to the winds through the two valleys — Romsdalen and Isterdalen—a change on the dry sand is perceptibly going on at all times. This is especially to be noticed at a spot called Gryten. In the maps it is marked as a church, and a church there once was in the position indicated; but, as we have already observed, it was so sanded up that it was taken to pieces and removed to Veblungsnæs away from the sand-storms, and just bordering on the fjord.

The tourist of the promiscuous class is sure to rejoice in this part of Romsdal, as here is situated an old farmhouse, now adapted to modern customs, and purveying comforts of all kinds not generally found in Norway. A friend, visiting this happy spot some twenty years ago, was kindly received by the proprietor, Herr Landmark, who is still spared to conduce more than ever to the increasing wants of Norwegian travellers. By degrees the farmhouse has developed, and is now, with its new *annexe*, generally spoken of as the "Hotel at Aak." Still, how different is it from the modern idea of such things! Very much of the leaven yet remains—

the same kindly reception, and the *likkelig reise* to the parting guest. Many
ask regretfully as they leave the entrance of the house—in itself a picture:
up four wooden steps to a stage with two small tables and seats—where
such is to be found; others, perhaps just arrived, feast their eyes on
the view over the Rauma towards the Drönningen and Biskop, in Isterdal;

The Farm at Aak.

while others, again, anxiously watch for the first peep of the Romsdal Horn.
Over the door and by the side clusters generally a glorious honeysuckle,
which grows most profusely, and adds much to the picturesqueness. Inside,
to the left, is the *salle à manger*, out of which leads a small room, which is,
I believe, now generally left for any ladies stopping in the house. Not
much monotony is there, but many delightful evenings, with a little music,

and sometimes an exceedingly good rendering of Mendelssohn, Schumann, Offenbach, or even the severe but sterling Beethoven.

One evening, after a very earnest attempt on the part of our coterie to sing some Norwegian songs by Kjerulf, it was discovered that amongst those listening outside was the brother of the composer, Professor Kjerulf, now of the Geological chair at Christiania. He expressed himself as being highly gratified with the English appreciation of his brother's undoubted talent. All this musician's work has great individuality and crispness, and his airs always "go" well. Hear his "Brudefærden."

BRUDEFÆRDEN I HARDANGER.

SUNG AT BUVALDEN AND THORBU-SÆTER.

Words by A. Munch.   Music by H. Kjerulf.

The Trollnderne by Moonlight.

The previous woodcut shows the north side of the house and farm-buildings. The *stabur*, or provision-house, is there, with the bell above. This bell is rung regularly for the farm labourers to come in, as they are always fed by the *bönder*, and the meals, though very simple, seem frequent. It was at this good hostelry that Lady Di Beauclerc stopped and described the French count who was in search of good "chase" of reindeer there, and the lady whose pursuit was *le saumon*, and who had a fly of the same colour as her costume. One becomes imperceptibly very curiously impressed by an association of ideas. Several people have mentioned that they felt rather surprised that they had never seen the count with his French hunting horn, nor the lady. There is still an idea that their ghosts linger about the spot, waiting, we suppose, for the reindeer and the salmon to come to them. The friend who was so kindly received here some twenty years ago was offered a little fishing by Herr Landmark. A portion of the river Rauma runs in front under the house, and the good sport made the happy fisherman rabid for life on salmon; he has been to Norway almost every year since, and taken many with him.

A few miles above Aak, leaving the sand plateau behind, we enter the Romsdal valley proper, with the Romsdal Horn rearing its grand peak on the left. The Troltinderne, or the Witches, is one of the most remarkable groups of fantastically jagged rocks in Norway, ever varying in effect, the mist wreathing and most delicately veiling or throwing a film over them, which makes them more gigantic and weird than ever. The outline of the peaks when clear is very serrated indeed, and with the Northern people a fair share of superstition attaches to them. These two elements have brought about the tradition that the series of *aiguilles* represent a wedding party going to the church. First, the *spilleman* (fiddler), then the *kinderman* (best man) with a tankard; the next large peak is the priest; then come two peaks, turning away as it were one from another: these were the unhappy bride and bridegroom, who foolishly and injudiciously quarrelled. Next come the father and mother. But the most curious character yet remains. By the side of a sharp point is a mass of rock, which certainly does look very much like a figure: this is the disconsolate lover, who, seeing that the bride and bridegroom had already quarrelled, makes a frantic rush to cut in and carry off the lady. This must have been the precise moment when they were all turned into stone, and so they remain, a warning to all frequenters of the valley. That the peasants believe in spirits and "little people" living on the fjeld, even in this year of grace, cannot be denied, as they say they do; but why they should think that these little people have blue heads I cannot imagine.

Exactly opposite to the Romsdal Horn, on the other side of the valley,

Meal House: Fiva, Romsdal.

is an immense *couloir*, originally an enormous landslip, leaving the perpendicular sides of the Troltinderne to gradually crumble and fall down, the finer stuff and *débris* filling up the interstices between the bigger rocks. After frost the thunder of the falling rocks and stones into this terrific shoot will last as long as thirty seconds, and the nightfalls create constant alarm to new-comers; whereas the *elve-wakker*, or river-keeper, merely remarks, "The old ladies are quarrelling," or "The old ladies have finished *aftenmad* and are throwing out the bones." Still, this brings about a new range of thought to a person who has never observed portions

of the earth's surface in motion. After seeing a huge rock, the size of
a stucco-faced villa, hop down the side of a mountain, there arise a certain
impressiveness and grandeur unknown before. About once a year there
is an important landslip in Norway—hardly more. Most of the loose rocks
have their regular grooves, and the peasants know how to avoid them;
still, as the vast country is so sparsely inhabited, many must occur which
do not "get into the papers." A curious instance of the effect of a small
landslip occurred in this valley to an old man personally known to us. A

The Louve at Fiva : Romsdal.

slip came down behind his house, of good timber stuff, and fortunately
stopped just short of it. He and his wife decided to leave, and go to live
at a place called Aalesund; they did so for a twelvemonth, after which
time they became home-sick, and, chancing all further damage, returned
to the old house, where they were living very happily last year. In another
part a description will be given of an important *steen-skred*—a scene of
terrible destruction and considerable interest.

The centre of the valley has two or three good farms, highly productive
for Norway, and presenting a very curious appearance to a foreigner

when the corn is cut, as the sheaves are stuck upon a pole, sometimes
five, sometimes ten, with the head facing the sun, and, as the sun works
round, the heads of corn are kept turned to it, so as to get the greatest
amount of heat, which is an advantage when the peasants arrive at
the happy time for carrying their corn, as they have only to pull up the
stakes with the five or ten sheaves on them, and they are easily carried.
Whilst on the subject of corn-drying, it is a most remarkable thing that
during the fine weather of the short Norwegian summer the wind helps

Rauma River Boat.

materially by blowing what the natives call a *sol-gang*: the wind goes
round with the sun all day, beginning to blow from the east in the morning,
due south at mid-day, and north-west in the evening.

Having paid especial notice to the Trols, we must turn to the Horn,
which rises on the left side: 4,000 feet is the height of it, and it goes sheer
up out of the valley; in fact, one morning, as we were sitting by the river,
a carriole came hurrying by, and a voice from it inquired, "Where's the
Horn?" The old fisherman with me stared at the flying folk in search of
information, and pointed straight up over our heads. The summit has

Romsdal Snow.

never been reached yet, either by the Government engineers who surveyed
the country, or by Alpine men, who have all given up the Aiguille Dru as
hopeless, or by captive balloon, which has been proposed. A very likely
party from a yacht made a bold attempt at it, but even some of these
looked upon it as a hopeless case, from the fact that there is a lean-to on a
huge shoulder on the north-west side. Perhaps the most beautiful time of
all to see this wild valley is after the first sprinkling of snow, when the tops
are powdered, which happens when the "iron days" come, the first snow
falling about August 20th. After a little sharp frost the weather recovers
from its first shudder, but by the 29th of September all is snow again
down to the river. Patches of old snow are always lying in the valley,
even during the hottest summer, but much more in the *couloir;* and, from
the immense scale of everything here, the real quantity
is most difficult to appreciate.

At the foot of this Romsdal Horn is the Rauma
itself, the first fall caused by the rocks thrown down
when the *couloir* was originally formed; and between
the river and the base of the Horn runs the road
through the valley to Gudbransdalen. There are a
few sheep here in the advanced farms, and these, like
all animals in Norge, are wonderfully docile. For
some time we heard sounds of music at a distance,
but could never discover either the music or the musician, until one day a
boy was found playing in a barn, or *laave,* on a goat's horn with six holes
in it, and with a reed mouthpiece. The sound is quaint. This instrument
was intended and used for the amusement of the sheep, and the boy's
mission was to play to them on it. The sheep and goats here always
follow instead of being driven; and, like all other animals in this country,
they are remarkably tame, never exhibiting the least signs of fear. This is
another pleasant feature resulting from the kindliness of the people and
their domestic happiness. Long may both remain to them!

The sight of the square-sailed craft with one mast and a bold rampant
black stem at once shuts out all intrusive thoughts of civilisation, for

these same vessels—relics of very old days—are seldom seen anywhere
save on the wild shores of Heligoland, working down to Bergen, or still
farther south round by the coast, and up to the town of Christiania.
These craft are mostly from the north of Trondhjem: their lines are very
fine indeed forward, the after part, with quarter-deck, forming a kind of
citadel for the captain. As these vessels come from the coast opposite
to the Lofoden, they are closely allied with the fishery of that district—the
great national fishing ground of Norway, to which rushes every able-bodied
fisherman from Bergen northwards as far as the North Cape. In the
month of February the fish are in force—principally early arrivals; and
ultimately such immense quantities are gathered together that tradition
has handed down to us as a fact that there are times when a deep-sea
line will hardly sink through them. Lines and nets are both worked with
the greatest system. The take is generally tremendous, and the results
lucrative. The fish are cured as stock-fish until April, when they are
split, salted, and dried on the rocks like Scotch cod. It is a simple process
to gut and hang up these cod-fish two and two across poles; not even salt
is used—nothing but the sea breezes, sun, and wind. Many years ago the
takes were even more enormous than at present, amounting to as much as
16,000,000 fish, or 8,000 tons dried, to say nothing of the cod-liver oil
and roe; but when we consider that these fish are gradually dispersed over
Europe, even 8,000 tons would soon go during the period of a continental
Lent. About April most of the fishers return home, and are ready for
any chance of herrings, which are as great a blessing to the Norwegians
as to the Scotch and Irish.

There was a very striking instance of an old custom in one of the outlying fjords, where the fashion of bygone centuries is still faithfully
kept up. At the entrance of the fjord is a boat, in which is stationed
the watcher, with a horn or bugle. As soon as the herrings are descried
the watcher, or rather the look-out, stands up in the bow of the boat and
sounds his horn. The notes are quickly caught by the anxious longing
ears on the beach, the boats put off, and soon the herrings feel that they are
"fish out of water," and will ere long be adding much to the happiness and
support of all the *bønder* and agricultural peasantry of the neighbourhood.

Making for the Fjord.

Near our herring scene was a well-to-do but scattered hamlet, for it could scarcely be called a village; and, having visited some of the good people, who were much interested in the foreigners—N.B., it is a curious sensation when it first dawns upon the mind of an Englishman that he is a regular foreigner in the eyes of others—we came to the conclusion that, all in all, the Norwegian *bönder*, as a class, are more comfortably provided with the good things of this world than any other of similar position. Their outdoor life brings sound health; they work hard, especially the women; and their reward is abundance. Their farms produce all they require to eat, drink, and even wear. In the fine weather they work for internal comforts; in the bad winter weather they provide for external wants in the form of carding, combing, and weaving in their houses, and making *vadmel*, or homespun—a material in which "shoddy" is unknown, and for which "everlasting wear" is the best name. They have their ponies, their boats, a wholesome love of God, and veneration for true, practical religion. Their houses are of their own building—sound, solid, and warm. There is no money greed amongst them, until spoilt by tasting the fruit of the tree of civilisation, and then the reaction is all the worse. Another great blessing that remains to them is, that there is no tendency to extravagance, no wish to launch out in competition with their neighbour. A peaceful, contented, simple life seems to them the *summum bonum:* this they possess, and are careful not to part with. Until savings-banks were introduced they really had no use for money, and when they acquired silver, instead of investing it, they had something new made of it, in this respect strongly resembling the old Dutch farmers, who were sometimes quite at a loss to know what they should have made next. The latter, indeed, went so far as to have candle-boxes, as well as other domestic utensils, of silver. Again, Norwegian servants are in good relationship with their masters and mistresses: much kindly feeling exists, coupled with a sense of duty and a proper regard for relative position, which is never forgotten.

We have mentioned the "home-madeness" of everything in a Norwegian farmer's house; but we have yet to refer to the woodwork supply, namely, sledges, agricultural implements, *stolkjars*, rakes, scythe handles, carrioles, tankards, teenas (written *tine*), butter-boxes, and bedsteads.

These last-mentioned items are the worst things produced in the country. The beds are all too short—never are they long enough. It seems as if the Norwegian has not quite grown out of the idea that in sleep the body should be bent up with the knees to the chin, and in the Isle of Skye tradition assigns to the Norsemen certain stone graves composed of nearly square slabs. The only way in which a tall traveller in Norway can avoid pushing his feet through the footboard is by bending his body up. The best carrioles are built at Drammen and Christiania, but they are advanced specimens, with springs; and springs are considered a little foppish, as well as liable to break, length of shaft being all the spring required. When these vehicles have to go on to steamers or large boats—a very frequent necessity, as the whole seaboard is constantly incised by fjords and arms of the sea—it is usual to take off the wheels, when the body is soon removed. Where rivers have to be crossed, and a small boat only can be procured, the best way is to bring the latter side on to the carriole, place a plank with one end on *terra firma*, and the other on the gunwale of the boat, where the wheel of the carriole nearest to the shore should ultimately go. The object of this is to run the wheel along on this plank to ship the carriole in the boat. This done, there is still a difficult part to be performed: the river has to be crossed, and if once the balance is lost, all is over. The rush of the river is very strong in parts, but even a kind of race makes no difference. A pull on one side, then a shoot and a pull on the other, and smooth water is reached, safety insured, and the carriole is over. Sometimes a river may be forded, but great care should be taken, as the want of local knowledge may in a moment cause a loss of life, or at all events a ducking.

We were once fording a river when Old Kyle, our blind dog, was travelling very comfortably in a dog-bag, or *hund sæk*, under the carriole. The excitement and novelty of the ford made us forget our old pet, and the first hint we had of his discomfort was the sorry sight of the dog vainly endeavouring to stem the current, while the only way of recovering him was by wading back. The carriole is used for everything; even the post-carrier is a carriole-driver, and is provided with a huge leather bag or portmanteau, with an iron rod running through it, and padlocked at the end. The postman carries a revolver, more as a staff of office or official status than anything else, for no one ever hears of such a thing as a robbery in this part of the world. The last few years have brought about a very great facility of communication in Norway, for which all travellers are much indebted to the energy of the Government. One can telegraph to any part of Norway for tenpence, and the stations are numerous—surprisingly so, when the extent of country and sparseness of population are considered ; and for

Shipping a Carriole.

English travellers the convenience is very great, because almost all the telegraph-station masters speak and write English well.

The woodcut (see page 55), with the sea-houses close to the water and *jægt* lying close in, shows the character of the country round that beautiful spot in the Hardanger fjord generally known as Rosendal, a place of great interest to the historian as the last seat of the Norwegian nobility. Nestling in a wood on the rising ground beyond the seashore lies this baronial residence, the home of the "last of the barons." Baron Rosenkrone still lives there, and in this secluded spot art has been cherished and loved, for Rosendal possesses a collection of pictures which is considered the finest in Norway. Who would expect, after trudging for nine hours over the snow expanses of the Folgefond, and rapidly descending on the Hardanger fjord, to find there such examples of highly civilised life?

Close to this point is the island of Varalsoe, famous for its sulphur mines. It lies out of the regular beaten track, but is sometimes visited by the *Argo* when the steamer is ordered to call for a freight. On such occasions the vessel is naturally light, and the first shoot of ore sent into the hold from the shipping pier above is, of a truth, a shock to the strongest nerves; the rattle and bang of the first few waggon or truck loads would startle any one, and make him fancy they would go through the ship's bottom and sink her. Not so, however: the people here understand their work, and it is not by any means the first time they have shot ore into an empty hold. May it not be the last!

Grassland, Meiboro(?)
i her heard.

HE Gudbransdalen valley is characterized by an immense *vand*, or lake, which is the source of the two rivers Rauma and Logen, the former running south-east, and the latter north-west into the Christiania fjord. Coming up from the Rauma valley, it was twilight as we reached the plateau of this upper valley, lying about 4,000 feet above the sea—a vast mass of far-stretching moorland, with heather, matted cotoneaster, and every variety of berry, in all the prismatic colour of the west coast of Scotland, but more vast, mysterious, and weird; and like witches looming moodily away from anything with life, we came ever and anon on some bleached relic of the grandeur of those noble Scotch firs which now seem fast fading away into mere skeletons and dried bones, the fibre in many cases appearing twisted like the strands of a rope, as though the dissolution had been one of agony and torture.

Soon after passing a monolith supposed to have been erected to the

Interior of Molmen Church.

memory of Sinclair and his Scots we approach Mølmen. Judging from its appearance on the map, any one would fancy it to be a town. Such, however, is not the case, for it merely consists of a church school, open on alternate Sundays, and a station, or farm, for the convenience of travellers. Within the last few years this station has greatly improved. We arrived late in the evening, and, feeling very chilly, huddled up to the fireplace. As we inquired from the *pige* what *aftenmad* we were likely to obtain, from the depths of the dimness of darkness muffled peals came from under a heap of "somethings" in a long parallelogramic case, but really a bed, containing the mistress of the house, and the muffled peals were to summon a supper for us, and quickly. So delighted were we get it, that we said "Tak for mad" before we began, instead of waiting till we had finished.

The church is of wood, larger than most Norwegian churches, and has a spire with four turrets, each with an elaborate weathercock. Mølmen must at one time have had weathercock on the brain, for there is one at the end of the roof, another on the top of the spire and on each of the turrets, and even one on the lych gate. This crop of ironwork is accounted for by the fact of there having been iron works at Lesje, some seven miles farther to the eastward. Passing through the lych gate, which is ponderous, the grave-boards attract attention from their variety; one in particular had the novel feature of a weathercock on the top, and at the back might be seen quite a contrast in sentiment—a small simple iron cross firmly mortised into the solid rock.

Entering the church, the general appearance is most striking, very quaint old carving, rudely painted—most comically rudely painted, especially on the rood screen, which is above—running from the pulpit to the two pillars in the centre, through which the altar is seen. The church floor is strewn with juniper tips, and the altar covered with a white linen cloth, whereon were two large candlesticks, which are lighted in the great festivals. The panels of the altar are painted in rather good colour, the back of it being of a slate colour; and, on the right side of it, standing back, is the carved stall for the use of the bishop when he visits the district. On the rood screen, over the centre, are the arms of King Christian V., with supporters, and above these a large but very uncouth figure of the Saviour on the cross, with I. H. S. above. On each side is a figure rudely carved and painted, as is the case with the pulpit. There are traces, too, of the delightful annual custom of these good people, who, when the summer bursts suddenly and joyfully upon them, and the flowers come rapidly out, cull the earliest, and take them to the church as first-fruits of thankful joy. After viewing the front of the altar we went round to the back of it—the Sanctum. This was a treat. There we found old silver chalices and curious cases for the sacred wafers; for these good people consider the form of worship immaterial, if the spirit be sound. The size of the wafer is about one inch and a quarter in diameter.

A very fine old vestment is still worn for the communion; it is richly brocaded, with a large purple cross on the back, and in the centre of this is a brass crucifix. The verger said it was a pity to have a new one until this was worn out. It certainly wears well, for it has been in constant use ever since the Reformation. The great feature, however, has yet to be noticed. A curious instrument is used as a persuader during the service: it consists of a pole, painted red, about eight feet long, with a knob at each end. On inquiring the use of this instrument and for what ceremonial, the verger, with surprise at our ignorance, said, "To wake the sleepers." How? "Here, sirs," continued he, placing his hand on his waistcoat, as indicative of the best place to tilt at effectually. The reader will be glad to know that the knobs did not betray much sign of wear.

We must now return to the station, which is associated with greyling in the river, and wood-carving executed during the winter months in the farmhouses—spoons, bellows, tankards, mangel brats, and culinary implements. It was our good fortune to meet at Mølmen a delightful Austrian—his grey and green jacket informed us of that fact—but his general information was an oasis for travellers. A great botanist, it was delightful to go out with him, especially as he was, at that moment, perfectly mad about saxifrages and the flora of Norway. Then, again, "flies." He had been up the North Cape, to the Namsen and other large rivers, and some one had given him a few Namsen "Butcher's"

salmon flies of immense size. These he showed to us; and we, finding him
so interested, asked him if he would like to see our collection of *natural*
flies. "Certainly." The flies we exhibited were the mosquitoes we had
shut up between the leaves of note-books when the flies had been thickest
in our tents on a warm evening. "Ah!" exclaimed our Austrian, "ten
tousand of dose fellows did I swallow at the North Cape, and they bite
all the way going down." Happily, however, he had survived. We also
met here a distinguished Prussian—large forefinger ring, *très Prussien*—
whose favourite exercise at the festive board astonished us. Mountain

A Norwegian Salmon Sta...

strawberries at Mølmen are a treat, and at dinner we had some. Our
aristocratic foreigner plunged them into a tumbler of sparkling wine,
but alas! how did he extract them? The Count must have been in a
lancer regiment, for with a tent-peg action he tried to pig-stick each
strawberry and raise it to his mouth with his toothpick, persevering
until the tumbler was emptied, and the last strawberry pierced and
entombed.

In passing along the shores of the fjords a kind of stage may be seen
occasionally, which would give the casual observer an idea of preparations

for pile-driving ; but the object of this construction is for quite a different
purpose.   It is one of the dreadful means used by the Norwegian farmers
to obtain salmon.   The system is this :—*Netting.*—A man sits in the
perch-box ; the net is laid round to the buoys as indicated in the previous
illustration, and, as soon as the fisherman (if he may be designated by that
name) sees a salmon underneath and within his net limit, he hauls in, and
generally gets him.   The salmon, being in the habit of returning to the
same river or *fos*, are sometimes the victims of an inquiring mind in
the following manner :—The Norwegian whitens the face of the rock, or
places a light plank so that the fish's attention may be attracted, and,
whilst making up his mind as to whether it may be right or wrong, his

Hardanger.

fate is sealed, and he will soon be hung up in the farmer's house, with
with two sticks across his body.   After it has been rubbed with sugar
and smoked in juniper fumes it is certainly a goodly adjunct to a breakfast ; but when the weary traveller finds only smoked salmon, he cannot
help thinking of the days when he was young, and had fresh meat
regularly.

    When coming down from the Haukelid Pass out of Sæterdal to the
Hardanger, we had not time or space to refer to a very beautiful passage
between the two, which we will now notice.   We came from Haukelid a
little gloomy ; we had seen a corrie which had been the scene of a reindeer
slaughter, or Glencoe, the result of misplaced generosity on the part of
an Englishman to a Norwegian.   The former had given the latter a

double-barrelled breech-loading rifle, with a good battue supply of cartridges. The consequence was that the local Nimrod, assisted by a confederate, drove a herd of reindeer into a *cul-de-sac* corrie, and then shot down more than twenty. This was worse than the friend who gave his river watcher a salmon rod and flies; the *elv-vakker*, or keeper, fished hard with fly and worm, and with much glee wrote to his lord and master in England that he had caught "plenty salmons, or *stor lax*," and the river would soon be ready for him, but he would like two new tops brought out for the rod so kindly given to him.

Journeying from Haukelid, we came down to Roldal, where the pass combines to produce a scene of great grandeur. The old wooden bridge, the blustering torrent falling with ponderous leap down into a chasm below, the serenity and peace of the distant snow range, and the placid lake far, far below, formed a combination which causes regret that it can never be adequately depicted on paper. The scenery is immensely grand, the living proportionately sparse and meagre. It is the old story, the quotation of Bennett's Guide-book—"Magnificent waterfall at back; only two wooden spoons at this station."

A tremendous zigzag is being cut by the Government in connection with a road which is ultimately intended to be opened over the pass. From the top of this zigzag a very commanding view is obtained of the valley of Seljestad and the Folgefond—an immense expanse of snow. We were very tired on arriving at Seljestad, and could get nothing but a recorked bottle of beer, which must have been put back several times on being declined by previous travellers. There was nothing to eat or drink; but such a *blakken*, or Norwegian pony, was put into No. 3 carriole, with the proprietor up as *skyds*. Having gone about five miles, the owner thought that the animal was not showing what he could do, or even up to his fair average; so, taking the rope reins, he stood up at the back of the carriage, grunted at him, and with deep growlings of "Elephanta!" sent him flying at a tremendous pace downhill, and, when far down the valley, we flew along the road through the spoondrift of two fine falls. The owner explained that the pony hated being called an elephant, and always went better when a little abused.

THE FJELD AND REINDEER.

THE FJELD AND REINDEER.

EVER and anon we arrive at some landmark in life which stands out prominently for the rest of our terrestrial journey. Perchance it is one that, surrounded with pleasant associations, invites us back to chew the cud of past happiness, and rises before us as an angel of comfort from time to time, when shadows, storms, or squalls of trouble cross our path, or the hurry-skurry of advanced civilisation has ruffled our calmer nature, and we have become irritable and over-strained, liable to spontaneous combustion of temper, and less kindly than usual. Such a happy landmark is "after reindeer" in Norwegian travel. Let us, then, look back to it, and enjoy it over and over again; and may others derive equal pleasure from similar outings!

The 1st of August is the opening day for reindeer-shooting. About the end of July the enthusiasm gradually increases, everything is supposed to be ready, lists are gone over, fine weather hoped for, and the 1st of August eagerly anticipated. On our way to Gudbransdalen we stopped at

Aalesund for the night; and what a night! We had hardly settled down to our *aftenmad*, or supper, before a servant came in to tell us of a grand sunset, which she thought the English gentlemen would like to see. We all rushed up-stairs, clambered through attics, and finally came out on a kind of platform; and what a sight met us here! The whole heavens were bathed in the most astounding crimson; at our feet lay the harbour of Aalesund, and on the horizon, out in the Atlantic, long ultramarine-purple islands. It was sundown in its most intense arctic grandeur, with a few golden scraps of cirri in the upper heavens. So impressed were we that we mused in silence; adjectives had no power of expression; and we tacitly admired with awe and reverence.

On our return to the table some Cantabs had just arrived, and finding we were compatriots, the all-prevailing subject of the latter days of July rose to the surface. "Were we going after reindeer?" was followed by a sort of mitrailleuse volley of cognate inquiries. They had heard of three Englishmen—did we know them? as they were anxious to meet them before starting. At last the suggestion was thrown out, "Had we not better go another time?" We thought not. Then they divulged the name of him they sought, and the Patriarch revealed himself, quoting the *Duke's Motto*, "I am here." General rejoicing, fraternity, and a *skaal* for good sport succeeded, and the next morning we all started off together by steamer for our happy hunting-grounds.

On July 31st we made our head habitable quarters on the high plateau of the Lesje Vand, and had time to enjoy the detailed study of the upper flora and berry varieties, which are numerous in this country. Thus:—

Tytteber .	Red, juicy berry.
Blaaber	. . . . . Blueberries.
Multeber .	Juicy, hard berry of raspberry form.
Kirseber .	. . Cherry.
Bringeber .	Raspberry.
Bjørneber .	Bearberry.
Winber, *Kirsber*	Currants.
Stikkelber .	. Gooseberry.
Solber	Black currant.
Jordber	. Strawberry.

The ponies were packed with their curious birch-twig saddles, waterproof sheets for cork bed, deer-skins and air cushions, provisions, a small spade to trench round the tents, cooking canteen—a great work most cunningly carried out by the Tentmaster—lint, chlorodyne, &c.; steel nails to screw into boots for ice-work, *rauters*, or mufflers, long flannel night-shirts for cold, blue spectacles for snow, a little glycerine, telescope, compass, &c. Our beds were made with Iceland moss, water-proof sheet, cork mattress, and skins, and we slept in thick socks, gloves, and long flannel night-shirts with hood to keep off the flies. Hans Luther was with us, and Trophas the faithful, the doggie with sharp nose and curled tail. The tents had been sent up to the fjeld before us, and, after about six hours' walk, we spied the white dot—the tent. In making the ascent to the upper plateau the gradual decrease of vegetation was very notice-able, culminating in the reindeer flower, or *Ranunculus glacialis*, which is much liked by the reindeer. Happy and buoyant with hope the hunter who finds the flowers nibbled off! Their peculiarity is to grow most freely where the snow has melted back. At the tents we found Ole

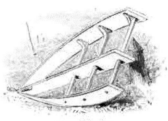

Snow Plough.

of Lesje, whose first news was that he had seen a herd of about fifty rein-deer, after which an important subject was mooted: a glutton had been seen the night before near the tent. Danjel Kulingen had been thirteen years after reindeer, and had never seen one. On the other hand, Hans Luther had shot one, and there was a skin at the station at Mølmen, which reminded us that at fishing inns on the banks of the Thames larger fish are seen stuffed and glazed than the itinerant angler generally hooks and lands.

All at once the dogs, three in number—Trophas, Barefoed, and Storm —opened a barking chorus; but we did not seize our rifles, as the tele-scopes revealed our Paymaster-general, who was returning from his *chasse de bagage*, which he had happily recovered. The aneroids registered 5,000 feet, and all was full of promise, save the one fact that the rifle of our friend was below in the valley. The despair and ferocity engendered by this unhappy discovery were soon dispelled by good food, and plenty of it, a word of comfort and sympathy, and last, not least, a little whiskey, after which he took a siesta in his tent, on which we wrote " Requiescat in pace," and left our cards as a welcome. Being Sunday, we made it quite a day of rest, and revelled in the flora, mosses, and lichens of our new ground, always, however, with an eye to the glutton, which evidently had a day of rest also, as he never appeared. In the evening, at 6.30, we had a hunters' chorus, for the Norwegian Sunday terminates at six o'clock.

NORGES HERLIGHED.

Words by I. N. Brun.

Vin og klare-rer Ud - gif - ter, Klippens Top som Gra - nen bar, muntre Sjæles

Fri - stel - er, Vo - dens Tummel ned-en-for til min sky - tøje Bo - lig ej naar.

Ole sang "Saga's Hall." Luther, with his sweet high tenor, was very good, and eventually a bouquet was thrown to him. The delicate attention seemed to be appreciated, although it was composed of straw and red labels from the tin cans of our preserved meats, &c. Then we had a bar or two of "God save the Queen," and so into our tents. The next day we made a long journey, with much snow and heavy winds. In the afternoon we had to swim the ponies through a river—a very pretty sight indeed—the only drawback being clouds of mosquitoes. They were perfectly awful, and no avoiding them. We were even thankful to think we should not have them at home for a continuance, for the remark that we should soon get used to them afforded no comfort.

At this altitude we found the ptarmigan sitting about. The shooting of these birds does not commence until August 15th, and they seemed to know that we, as Englishmen, would not shoot before that day. So we actually threw stones at them, and one old bird, when knocked off the top of a large stone, positively came back to see what it was all about. Soon after this we discovered *friske spor* (new deer slots). The dogs livened up for a time. All soon settled, however, into steady travel again. Danjel was telescoping continually, but frequently a supposed reindeer turned out to be only a stone in the snow, till at last the Patriarch ventured to remark that there were "mange stor steen in

Gamle Norge, og maget god telescope jagt," which Danjel understood
to suggest real deer instead of stones, and we should all have preferred, as it was one of the objects of our expedition, shooting reindeer
to telescoping them.   They are very wild, and quite justify the old
saying, " Mange dyr, mange øine" (many deer, many eyes).   Our course

Snow Pass ; Thorbyu.

now lay from Buvalden due north, and we started in good time from
Thorbyu for the snow ranges, leaving the horses and baggage below,
we going as light as possible, with our own food for the day, and plenty
of goat cheese.   At lunch Danjel explained to the Patriarch that he
should eat much goat cheese, for if he eat sufficient he should partake
of the nature of that saltatory animal, and in time jump cleverly and

boldly from rock to rock—an accomplishment in much requisition during our wanderings.

An incident of piscatorial interest occurred here. We sent a hunter, who had never had a rod in his hand before, down to a lake, or *vand*, to try for some trout. In an hour he came back with about twenty, averaging nearly one pound each. Of course he was not casting, or "flick" would have been the fate of the fly; he only trailed. Still his success was perfect, and he was delighted with his new sport.

The male reindeer are called *bucks*, the female *ko* and *semle ko*, and the young *kalve*. In the daytime they roll in the snow, and if they sleep at all, it is certainly with one eye open. Having seen and telescoped many large stones, and taken them for deer, there was a strong inclination to inquire more closely as to the probability of sport, and a suppressed anxiety to hear a definite opinion as to our chance of a shot, if nothing more. The hunter must be patient, persevering, careful not to appear even as a moving speck on the interminable expanse of virgin snow, and take his sport quietly, for better or worse. Our Tentmaster had made many expeditions, had seen many deer, and even when his chance came an impetuous —shall we say friend?—rushed out in front of him, fired, and missed. So tradition said. We are glad to state that this did not occur during our present trip. His successes arrived, however, after a time, and never will he forget the day when he killed his first reindeer. Long may he live to kill more !

Let us here give his first experience; so pray silence for the Tentmaster.

THE TENTMASTER'S FIRST TRIP, AND HOW HE TRIED TO GET A REINDEER.

"In the year 1863 I ascended the glorious Norwegian fjelds for the first time to hunt reindeer. What a charm is conveyed in these words, 'first time!' The first salmon or trout caught; the first grouse or partridge shot; the first meet at cover and burst with the hounds; the first climb up the snow peaks of Switzerland; the young beauty's first London season,

or first night at the opera or ball; and last, not least, first love, all have
a peculiar zest never afterwards equalled."

(N.B.—The Tentmaster is rather sentimental.)

"I experienced this feeling in August, 1863, when, journeying up the
magnificent Romsdal valley, on arriving at a station I noticed a splendid
head of reindeer horns lying outside the station-house.   On inquiry I
found that a Norwegian hunter had brought them down from the fjelds.
I lost no time in searching him out, and soon arranged for an expedition

After Sport.

together. I had no provisions, tents, spare clothing, or other appliances
which my subsequent experience has shown to be requisite, but began
the ascent with the meagre store of some raw coffee berries, *flatbrod,* cheese,
and biscuits. The hunter (Dan I call him) could not speak English, nor
I Norske; but we got on pretty well by pantomime. After a pleasant but
toilsome three hours' walk through the grand scenery peculiar to the
Norwegian fjelds, Dan's hound Passop (the reindeer hounds are held in
a leash two or three yards long) suddenly squatted down in great excitement, with his nose steadily pointed to a huge rock about three hundred

Near Ösendal : efter Reimher.

yards distant, and gave a peculiar low whine. Dan was down immediately, and signalled me to do the same. He was certain that reindeer
were close at hand, but a full half-hour's telescoping failed to disclose
their whereabouts. Nothing could induce Passop to move; his sniffing
nose kept steadily in the direction of the rock; while he occasionally gave
us a most intelligent, imploring look, as much as to say, ' Do something.'
Unable to see any trace of deer, we dare not move. Dan thought that
wherever they were, there they would remain some time; so, with faithful
Passop on the watch, we determined to have lunch. Not a bite, however, would Passop touch—not even *flatbröd* thick with butter. There he

An Anxious Moment.

squatted, with his nose still to the rock, the model of a watchful sentinel.
Lunch finished, Dan began telescoping, and soon discovered the cause
of Passop's agitation. The tips of antlers were visible above the rock,
and in distinct relief against the sky. They were perfectly motionless;
but we were quite sure, after many exciting inspections with the telescope,
that a large buck was resting behind the rock. As the wind was not very
favourable Dan said we must be quite still, and remain till we saw a
movement. In my innocence I wished to smoke a pipe, but Dan forbade
it. The excitement was increased by Dan saying it was a large buck,
probably an outlying sentinel, and that a herd of deer was not far off,
which proved correct. Our patience being exhausted, Dan, much to the

delight of Passop, ordered a forward crawling movement; and, with time
and patience, we got within eighty yards of the rock, where we determined
to halt and wait. The tops of the antlers were still motionless. Poor
Passop was trembling with excitement, and his companions much the
same. In this position another half-hour passed, when suddenly Dan
exclaimed, 'Look!' Passop became very uneasy, when we had the pleasure
of seeing a splendid *stor buck* rise up and stand before us broadside, with
his head turned to where we were crouching. Passop behaved splendidly,

Hunter's Encamping.

remaining perfectly still, while I shall never forget the expression of his
eyes, and his occasional side glance at us, as much as to say, 'Now then.'
Resting my rifle on a convenient rock, I took aim steadily behind the
shoulder, pulled the trigger, and, to my horror, it missed fire. The buck
heard the snap, and started off at a rattling pace; Passop struggled wildly
to get out of the leash; and Dan exclaimed, 'Gud bevar mig! Give me
my rifle.' I handed it to him, he recapped it, and fired at about two hundred yards' distance without effect. Passop collapsed, and the translation
of his thoughts into English was indicated by the expression of his face,

'I have done my best!' No doubt he had a clear conscience; and work being finished, he commenced eating *flatbröd* and butter with great zest. The inevitable pipes were now brought out for consolation. Wonderful weed—exquisite after a success, soothing after a defeat!

"We now made our way to a stone cave to pass the night, where we had coffee and *flatbröd*. The cave was just large enough for me to creep in, and I passed the night on dried moss, sleeping soundly till daybreak. The night being very fine, Dan took up his quarters outside the cave, had coffee, and slept soundly on dried moss too. After breakfast we started,

Leaping down the Precipice.

Dan being sure we should find the herd. At one o'clock we discerned them, fourteen in number, taking their noonday siesta on the snow; but in vain we tried to get within shot. Next day we saw herds of deer, but without being able to get within range on account of the quantity of snow. On the third day I returned to the station, much delighted with my first reindeer-hunting experiences. Often as I have been on the fjelds since, the three days of 1863 have not been surpassed, although

NO DEER WAS KILLED."

It would be well here to say a few words respecting the tents and their arrangement.

A regular _tente abri_ carries two very well. Of course there are more room and comfort for a single inhabitant; still, for general travelling, in which luggage may only too truly be described as _impedimenta_, the tent referred to may be used. Every morning, if the weather permits, the waterproof sheet and cork bed should be laid out to dry, and the skins also. The trench round the tent must be well looked to, the lines tightened, and the ponies tethered, as it is rather disagreeable to be awakened about two A.M. by a storm of rain and wind, and to discover your pony, with his linked fore-legs well tangled in tent lines, doing his best to pull down the whole concern on the heads of the occupants. Far more delightful is it to be aroused on a bright, crisp, and fresh summer morn-

The Graileck.

ing, when, if near a _sæter_, the cause of it may be the jodelling of a _pige_ in charge of the cows—Swiss as to character of song, exceedingly Norske as she calls to them to follow. In the country districts animals follow more frequently than they are driven. Kindliness is the rural, coercion the town influence.

Many of our readers will notice that under the initial letter at the commencement of this chapter, the powder-flask and general arrangement are very much like the old bandoleers still hanging in the guard-chamber of Hampton Court Palace and others at Portsmouth. They were most general in Charles I.'s time, and are beautifully shown in De Gheyn's costumes of Culverin-men and Harquebusiers. In this case the bandoleer was made of steel, and it is faithfully rendered, with the cord by which the whole arrangement was hung over the shoulder of the hunter.

By this time we deserve sport. We have travelled far and worked hard for it. Let us see the result. We had arrived at a great height, at the snow-fields called Sneebreden, like the Folgefond in the Hardanger. We had slid, crawled, and struggled, sometimes moving one behind the other at an angle to reduce our surface, creeping on the crisp, dry, hard snow, wading rivers of snow-water (very cold tubbing indeed), sloshing at

Mind Notes.

the edge of the snow, where the reindeer-flowers bloom, and going through various other incidents of snow travelling, till at last we arrived at a smart drop, previous to another *fond*. Here the Patriarch had to be eased down, and his pendent position is only suggested in the cut (p. 147). Soon Trophas began to draw upon some slots in the snow, and it was the unanimous opinion that they were "fresh." Trophas pulled hard, held back by Ole, who eventually began to half trot. To the unsentimental mind the action was that of a blind man's dog eyeing coppers in the distance; but Trophas was in earnest, and at last the top of a horn burst upon us, and in a second our fate was disclosed to us. There was nothing but the gralloch of a reindeer *kalve* shot yesterday—one horn, one hoof, &c.—as shown in the sketch (p. 148). How could it be accounted for? Many suggestions were thrown out, many improbabilities considered feasible, and at last a matter-of-fact mind launched the frightful proposition that the glutton seen by Ole near our tents the night before our arrival was nothing but a native hunter, who had been stalking us, and had killed the *kalve* of which the remains were now at our feet. Nothing daunted, we flattered ourselves that at all events we had now commenced in earnest, and remembered the saw that the worst beginning has the best ending.

RAVELLERS in Norway are surprised, as they pass through the valleys, to see so few cows. This is easily explained. They visit this interesting country when these animals are away, like themselves, for a holiday; and as every dog has his day, so every Norwegian cow has her outing, and goes to the grass pastures in the upper plateau to enjoy life until the white mantle of snow is ready to garb the upper ranges and drive the cows and *piger* down to their homesteads and winter quarters. As already described, these *sæters*, or *châlets*, are high up, and frequently afford the energetic nature-loving traveller and genuine hunter cover and shelter, we may almost say comfort—*cum* very much *grano*, though. In snow-work it becomes almost luxury to have one of these to fly to in very bad weather.

Tent life is the most truly enjoyable thing—though there are times when a tent may be blown down and soaked through—to say nothing of the milk supply at hand, which is meat and drink at all times, although very filling at the Norwegian price. This will account for our associating a *sæter* so prominently with our snow-work. The one given in our woodcut (p. 149)

was inhabited by Maritz, who was there by herself from July to the beginning of September or end of August, according to the early or late fall
of the snow. The 20th of August generally brings the first fall of snow in
this latitude (63). During our stay we always slept in our tents, as we all
feared the parasitical ticklings the *sater* would inevitably have afforded us
had we given it the chance. All the summer through the old snow lay
round the antiquated wooden building, and seldom indeed was it that Maritz
had any one to speak to, as there was no road or path of any kind. Still
she was all kindness. Did she not send a pair of cuffs to the Patriarch's
wife, and iron them, so to speak, after her manner, with the back of a
wooden spoon, as she hummed a plaintive ditty in the minor key? Perhaps she thought the lady would hardly like to wear them, or else that
they might find their way to some great people. Maritz, too, held to the
superstitions of her ancestors. Thus her porridge swizzle-stick—which is
like the West Indian swizzles, but larger—made from the five-shoot top of
a young fir, was always prepared with a cross cut at the end or swizzling
part of it, to keep the Evil One from turning the milk sour. This, too,
she sent with the cuffs.

A little outdoor shed, or *laave*, was our general cooking-place, into
which four of us sometimes squeezed, and, as the dogs filled up the
interstices, we were as closely packed as sardines, the whole being seasoned
with the oil of good fellowship. It is wonderful how invigorating this life
is. What a system for a sanatorium! How well balanced should one
become with such fresh air, simple food, and exercise, and with all the
energy and toughness requisite for this work! It is inconceivable how
kindly, obliging, and tender towards others a life like this makes us.
Such was the influence of our head-quarters. Prosiness must be avoided,
however; so another day on the snow with the hopes of sport, and no
buck fever if we get a chance. Bad landmark that, if perchance it befall
us. We hope it will not: if it do we will forget it.

For our line the shortest way would be across the *vand* where the
trout were caught, and Danjel reported the discovery of an old boat of
that class which has no iron nails about it, but all wooden pegs, and yet
not particularly inviting as to safety, as the baling-ladle of birch wood

gave the idea that whoever last used it thought it would be wanted by
the next comer. However, as the hunters were agreeable and we could
all swim, we determined to try it. So off we started, with ominous
gurglings and washings to and fro in the bottom of the boat, fast,
frequent, and furious. The ladle was heartily plied, first by one strong
arm, then by another; but still the water came. This brought to our
remembrance the Scottish Highland custom of baling the boat with

A Friend in Need.

a good large shoe, and that if you only take a pair the power becomes
doubled.

Happily we arrived safely, and soon started for a long day's work over
unknown ground. The weather had cleared, and everything seemed to
combine in our favour. There was a hearty good spirit among our
hunters and ourselves, each fellow wishing the other good sport, and the
dogs were keen to a degree. They longed for a revenge after the affair
of the old gralloch, and flattered themselves that, if we were not unlucky,
they would get fresh blood before nightfall. We were soon beginning
to ascend steadily, and about an hour after starting, the Patriarch, working

his way under some overhanging rocks, met with a surprise. An eagle, a large specimen, swept over his head and shadowed him. With his rifle in its case and across his back, the noble bird was safe, and the Patriarch delighted. Must there not be a nest? Yes, there was. Rough sticks and the lightest of down feathers were all that it was made of—rude, simple, and, one would think, uncomfortable for so grand a bird.

The Eagle's Nest.

Some of the down feathers were taken as a souvenir, and now and then brought out and floated, so light are they, in recollection of our having found one of the noblest of birds at home.

By mid-day we were out on the open snow, with hardly any rock shelter for stalking, should fortune favour us. The reindeer, however, were not "at home;" so we stopped at a suitable rock for lunch. How we enjoyed it! Old Trophas wagged his tail with a conviction that "no sport, no food," would never be his fate as long as there was something left in our wallets. So we all rejoiced together, winding up with a little whiskey and hearty wishes for good sport.

Soon after lunch the tips of some horns were just visible on the snow-line. A large expanse of snow lay before us, with some small rocks half-way. Could we reach them? No; so we waited for the chance of the deer working up our way. Unfortunately they moved in the opposite direction, and our chance was gone. Still we had seen some, and that inspired fresh hope. Later in the afternoon we again saw a herd, and

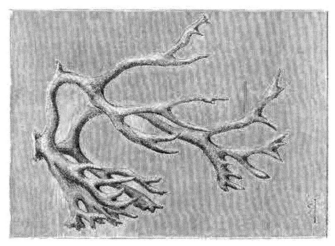

Reindeer Head.

telescoped them for a length of time. Soon after this a second herd became visible, and it was most interesting to watch their manœuvres, which we did until they joined and moved off—of course in the opposite direction. An immense expanse of snow was now before us, and once we saw four herds of reindeer, and could count about one hundred and forty. For a long time we had hope, and agreed that if we could only get one we should be satisfied; but even that was denied, for the four

* This head, of forty-one points, is in the collection of Sir Charles Mordaunt, Bart., at Walton Hall.

herds gradually blended and went straight off, leaving us in the most perfect solitude, reindeerless.

By this time we had a long distance to travel to get back to our tents. Fortunately the light fades so little that it hardly signifies; still great care is required to judge of the best footing after leaving the snow, as the hunter leads, and can go any way, even to rolling down places like a hedgehog, and sometimes sitting down for a slide. Indeed, going home becomes a kind of steeple-chase over unknown ground. In such cases woe and grief must be the fate of the novice. At the highest elevation

Red Deer Head.

we passed an immense boulder, very much like the Logan Stone, and of similar dimensions, though perhaps larger. On the top of this was a much smaller one, but of different geological formation. This gave rise to considerable discussion about the glacial theory, as there was a non-believer present. What could have produced this remarkable combination but the action of glaciers passing over the surface, bearing huge masses of rock from distant parts, and, as the ice melted away, depositing them? These boulders were found at an elevation of 5,000 feet or more. We also met with a most interesting instance of pink snow, very marked indeed in colour. All these varied phases of nature did much to repay us for our disappointment respecting the deer. This the difficulties of the descent also made us for the time forget, as Danjel Kulingen was tearing away as hard as he could possibly go, sometimes letting himself down, then hanging on to the undergrowth of heather, sliding, rolling, or jumping. We often solaced ourselves with the idea that if we could only get him on the flat for ten miles for a finish, we could give him a spin and run him in at high speed.

Whilst we had been telescoping the deer our Aalesund friend was having sport. On our return we found that he had been over to our tent to see us, and had left word of "Sport, sport," and a message to try for a meet. This, unfortunately, could not be arranged, or we should have seen joy depicted on his face when he described to us where and how he killed his first reindeer.

The Norwegians believe that the horns of the reindeer, boiled down, are good for consumptive people. There is no doubt that the reindeer themselves eat, or rather gnaw them when they are shed, which occurs in November. The males shed their horns first, the females retaining them longer. We found several horns partially gnawed through, and, when we consider the number of deer, there must be some reason why the shed horns are not more frequently picked up. The same idea of horn soup for consumptive cases occurs in Scotland, where the horns of red deer are also found gnawed. One would imagine that the best time for this *potage* would be when the horn was first formed, and the "velvet" is on, or when the horn is being renewed; and during this period it is very warm indeed, as large arteries run inside the velvet, or horn skin, and are engaged in depositing bone on the old stems, until the horns are complete and the velvet fretted off in September.

The reindeer, like ptarmigan, become white during the winter, and in their wild state present a great contrast to the sheeplike tameness of those possessed by Laplanders. The Laps have a regular call for their tame deer, which generally come at once; but if not, the proprietor has generally his lasso with him, which is thrown over the animal's loins, and he is at once a prisoner. The good travelling pace of reindeer is well known, being about ten miles an hour, with two hundred pounds weight at their back. In their wild state their pace was beyond computation when we were behind them. We could well say that we had been " after reindeer," and that is all. The only way to have sport in such a country as Norway is patiently to settle down to it, without fixing a time for returning. A river is not always right, nor the water in condition. So is it with the reindeer hunter: a thousand things may occur to mar his success. The very wind is sometimes wrong, and may chop round at the moment when he hopes it will hold on steadily for an hour or two; while, on the other hand, it may change at some fortunate moment exactly in his favour. No; there is no royal road to such sports as these. The charm of uncertainty must at all times attach to real sport. It must be worked for, and directly the uncertainty is removed its real charm is gone, and the relish for it dissipated. The mere act of shooting and killing lasts but a second of time; it is the surroundings which afford the real pleasure—the fresh air, the change of scene, the care required in every detail, the sportsman never knowing but that the very next moment some interesting incident may transpire which would make the day, hour, and spot a landmark; the necessity for watching every breath of air, the most delicate zephyr being registered and measured by the painstaking hunter, as he brings out tenderly some carefully preserved pieces of the finest floss silk, or, better far, some of the eagle's down feathers already alluded to. Again, the dogs require constant attention; and, to be quite complete, a coronet of eagles' eyes—optical all-rounders—would be an assistance.

ISHING for salmon, and the love which Englishmen have for that grandest of all sports, have led to the opening up of Norway to the general traveller. Our first pioneers, finding how importunate were the inquiries of the new-comers respecting the best spots and methods for sport, and that the inclination of some led them to try and bid above others for the waters they had really well earned by their own energy and perception—all this, we say, tended to make men on board the good ship *Tasso* rather *taciturn*. (Excuse the approach to an unintentional pun.) This, however, is not surprising, for men are compelled to be reticent when they know the inevitable consequences of giving details of their sport. Nothing will secure success but earnest work, patience, and biding your time for the happy combination which the best rivers can only afford now and then. Why, as we have just observed, the whole charm of sport would be dispelled if it became a dead certainty, and a man knew he would kill so many pounds of fish one day, and none the next. No; like the glorious uncertainty of cricket and hunting, the uncertainty of fishing is one of its charms; the average of good and bad is equalised, and the old French proverb comes in, that "Patience et longueur de temps font plus que la rage." The noble salmon has become liable to increased and more subtle dangers within the last few years, besides his old natural enemies. The peasants have new means of torture. His natural foes are the bull-trout and sea-trout, which are the vermin of every river, destroying the spawn wholesale, and even lying in wait for the moment when the female deposits her milt, an instance of which came under our observation. The nets at the mouth of the river are an old institution, but they should be well constructed and supervised; also the *tine*, or stage, described in a former chapter, where the *bonde* is anything but the "sweet little cherub that sits up aloft;" still it is an old custom, and we like old customs. So also is the "worm box" which hangs from the peasant's belt as he goes for some trout, or anything else that may be tempted. The worm box is a very primitive construction, its simplicity being well carried out in the birch twig by which it is suspended, and the two pieces of leather through which the lid slides. It is a picturesque relic of old days.

We now approach the recent diabolical invention of the "otter," which, sad to relate, must have been introduced thoughtlessly by some one who little knew what damage he was doing when, for his own selfish gratification, he fell back upon so unlawful and unsportsmanlike an expedient. Even to obtain food such poaching is unjustifiable. Certainly enough could have been taken for that purpose by fair means. It is of no use, however, dilating upon this; the deed is done, and otters cannot be withdrawn now. If the arm of the law were stretched forth, "les pommes volées" would become more than ever "les plus douces." Then, again, the kindly feeling engendered by good sport and a certain sense of gratitude frequently leads, at the end of a visit, to a gift of flies, perhaps even of a rod. In illustration of this let us repeat the case of the proprietor of a river who gave to Nils, his *iks-wakker*, a salmon

Worm Box.

rod and flies. Early in the season Nils began to avail himself of the new fishing-gear, and soon wrote home to his benefactor to say that the salmon were coming up the river, but that he had broken both tops of the rod, and lost most of the flies; would the gentleman kindly send out some more flies and tops to get the river ready for him? We do not think this was done; it could hardly be expected that any man would like all the salmon he killed to be landed with more than one fly, perhaps one in his mouth, one in each fin, and finally one in his tail. What an awful apparition for even the merest tyro! Such liberality is simply mistaken kindness. This brings to mind other stories concerning salmon-fishing.

It is often remarked that "truth is stranger than fiction." When an M.P. fishing in Scotland played and held his fish all night, and on the

following morning lost him, and a friend of his afterwards killed a salmon
with one of the M.P.'s favourite flies in his tail, that was certainly an
event, but hardly to be compared with what we are about to relate.   In
the large rivers of Norway a fishing may extend four miles, and the
fishing next to that only three, so that different waters are let to different
persons.   In the present instance our foreign Izaak Walton was fishing
the very top water, and, as good luck would have it, hooked a *stor lax*,
perchance a forty-pounder.   He played him firmly and steadily, but the

Fresh Fish at Dinner.

fish after a time got the gentleman at the reel end of the rod through
the next water and the next.   Hours rolled on, yet still down they went,
and by the next morning arrived at a shallow part of the river.   A
Norwegian peasant came up, and, despite the national dislike to going
into the water, plunged into the river, and walked out with the *stor lax*
in his arms—DEAD, and reported that he must have been dead for the
last five hours.   Nevertheless he got him, and a fine fish he was, with one
fly in the right place.

The Slipr-stone, or Ladder Rock.

The Norwegians have a great admiration and respect for a good fisherman. One morning, speaking of the average sport of the river, and referring to that of last year, we inquired if —— were a good fisherman. Knut answered emphatically, "No; he is a poor man, a very poor man." We naturally replied, "But in England he is a very rich man." "Ah!" said Knut with strong emphasis, "when he was here he was no richer than we, but the flies bite him much more." What contentment! no envying, although a latent satisfaction creeps out, which decidedly evinces an undercurrent of thought.

Trout-fishing has the great charm of taking Piscator into the most lovely and retired spots. The salmon, as a larger fish, takes us to a grander scale of nature. The water of the cheerful little trout stream is changed for the rushing river, and the comparatively low bank sometimes gives place to a position like that in the annexed illustration, which was taken from above a grand pool, the Stige-steen, or Ladder Rock, connecting it with the side of the river.

Having said somewhat of fishing, let us now turn to the "aldermanic view" of the salmon, and hark back to a happy day when a lady had killed a nice fish, about fourteen pounds and a half, which was to be cooked on the spot; it is well to observe the process and make a note thereof. Cut the salmon in slices, and boil them for ten minutes; then let the water in which they were cooked boil on, with the head added; put in a little fresh butter, pepper, and salt, and serve as gravy or sauce. With a Norwegian appetite it is perfect, and very simple. N.B.—Fish killed at noon, served at two P.M. This is fresh fish, and contrasts most favourably with the frozen salmon which travels ice-bound to the metropolis of Great Britain.

Evening is the best time for fishing, and the long twilight, which helps the enthusiast for trout and salmon fishing at eleven or twelve, can only be realised by those who know the glories of the North. It seems a curious thing to take, when travelling, a green blind in order to exclude the light when wishing to go to sleep; still it is necessary at first, although Nature is so elastic that she readily adapts herself to circumstances, when the green blind can be given to some new-comer, or lent as a passing boon.

One word in reference to the illustration, "A Good Beginning." It was our last morning: wind, rain, mist low down—in fact, blowing hard.

Casting.

No. 3 was up at five A.M., and found the Tentmaster-general had passed a restless night, every coverlet and blanket being knotted, twisted, and

twined into the most perfect disorder.   This was attributed to the fact
that it was his last night that season in Norway, and his usually placid
sleep had been disturbed with Norske nightmare.   He must have been
dreaming of trolds and *nökken*, and fancied that he was gaffing ogres or

A Good Beginning.

bjergtrolds instead of fine clean fish.   The weather was the last straw
which broke the camel's back—he would not go.   "You go," was his
rejoinder.   So the Patriarch went; and this was the result to greet his
companions when they came down to breakfast.

HERE is a great charm about the freedom of driving one's own pony and carriole, or *stolkjær*, for a long run, or even for a short excursion; it conduces to the peaceful rest we are all longing for, and saves one from reminders that at the next station the horses will be charged for if we do not hurry on. This is rather tantalising when one is drinking in nature, and realising the fact that each moment is revealing fresh beauties and developing lifelong impressions—the very time when one wants to be left to nature and himself. In the excursion now before us we had our own ponies part of the way, and pedestrianism for cross country. Our route was from Romsdal, the weird valley where, on the previous evening, the trolds had been playing pranks in the following manner:—About 8.30 a tremendously heavy roll as of thunder, lasting forty seconds, brought us suddenly to the window. The mist was hanging round the peaks, with cirri-strati across them; down came the *steen-skred*, or slip, with a mighty rush; and the cloud was driven out by the shower of rocks and stone as they came madly down. It was unusually grand. The sheep boy with his horn ran in, Anna rushed to the door to see it, and as she came the dust rose up in a cloud as incense after Nature's work. Ole remarked that it was a fine shower, and very impressive it certainly was; still Anna said she did not like it. In some cases in the winter-time the peasants go on to the ice to avoid the possibility of these erratic masses reaching them.

We were soon off to Gudbransdalen, calling as usual at Fladmark— that lovely spot, beautiful to a degree if you have provisions. Should such be the case, you certainly must have brought them, for the station is not one of refreshment, as Mrs. Brassey testified by her anxiety to regain her yacht, the *Sunbeam*, which is truly a sunbeam to her friends. Long may it be so to her and her husband and son!

We must leave the hurly-burly of rocks through which the Rauma dashes in this part. Rocks the size of detached villas seem to have been "chucked" about, for this is the only term we can bestow upon such higgledy-piggledy positions. One can only realise the idea by imagining one's self a minute insect in a basin of lump sugar, with a great rushing river beneath.

Arriving at Mølmen, we found it a most healthy spot, and worth staying at for a time, as the people are so kind, and the whole surroundings inviting. Being on a high plateau, the air is perfect, and the place seems to be more than usually fortunate in its weather. The following morning, there being no service at kirk, we availed ourselves of the perfect weather for enjoyment on the hillside. Striking off from the houses, we sauntered up through the stunted birch and the heather till the grey rocks became more prominent, the vegetation sparse, the plants closer to the ground, and then we lay down on the fjeld side. What a view there was beneath us! The whole scene was a rare combination of all the prismatic colours so characteristic of Scotland in October. At our feet was the long Lesje Vand, beyond that the Dovre fjeld, and we fancied we could see Snehatten; then, away to the right, were snow ranges to Storhættan, which is ascended from Ormem. How we basked in the sunlight and longed

for more life on the fjeld! "Why should we not go to Eikesdal?" said Ole all at once. "That would be fine: why not?" The idea was caught at. "How long would it take to walk, Ole?" "Well, eighteen hours if there is no mist." "Very well, then; no mist, if you please, and we will do it." This was a new joy: eighteen hours' walk without a house to call at, carrying one's own nosebag, and great doubts as to a bed on arriving— more delightful still! This is enjoyment indeed, though not to every one, perhaps. We therefore decided to start the next morning at three A.M., provided there was neither mist on the mountains nor the chance of it. How we revelled on the journey in anticipation, enhanced as our happiness was by the beauty of the scene and the grandeur of the surroundings! All the way down we conversed on our coming walk, interrupted only by a visit

to a farm, where we heard some of the good folk singing. It was hay-time;
the weather fine, with a refreshing breeze that gently waved the new-cut
grass as it hung from the frames, like huge towel-horses, which are used
for drying it. We were invited to enter the farmhouse, where we found
the room tidied up for Sunday, and the family singing a hymn in their
customary devotional manner. There was the usual three-cornered cup-
board; an old gun which had laid low many a good buck, the powder-flask,
primer, and ball-bag were ready for August; the ivy was carefully trained

up the windows inside; and the ale-bowls
and tankards were about the room. It was
quite a Norwegian homestead. One thing was
unusual—a musical instrument called a *psalmo-
dicum*, which is a board painted green with
red flowers, about an inch thick and thirty
inches long, with three strings raised on a
bridge like a violin. These strings are played
with a bow, also of the violin class, but different
in character. We regretted very much that we
could not persuade any one to perform upon it.

On our return we found the proposed trip
emanated from the fact that a house-painter
was going over to Eikesdal, and had been waiting for clear weather to carry out his object.
By the next morning a farmer from Eikesdal
proposed joining us: he knew the way. This

Wool Holder.

completed our party, and at four o'clock we started, with every assurance of
fine weather. Working up through the stunted birch-trees, we soon looked
over the heights of the Vermer Fos to Storhættan. The Svart-hø rose behind
us, and approaching the snow-line, we came upon the reindeer-flower (*Ranunculus glacialis*, with its sharp-pointed leaves and beautiful white blossom.
Then the dreary Gravendal opened to us, wild, bleak, weird, and barren to
a degree, with Amra Jura on our right, directly over Eikesdal, far, far
away. About this time there was a grand solar rainbow. We now got
very rough rock-tramping—regular *couloir* climbing—and there was no

vegetation, the moss being of the "crottle" tribe, a perfectly black lichen. As we ascended the peaks were grander. Many reindeer *spor* were seen, but no reindeer. At the highest part we found the snow discoloured by a very fine dark gritty dust ; and it is a remarkable fact that this discoloration was the result of volcanic eruption in Iceland. After the eruption a gale set in from the W.S.W., which on Easter Monday, 1875, positively carried the clouds of scoriæ right across Norway. The line was followed even to Sweden, and corroborated by some peasants who were out when it fell.

A volcanic eruption in Iceland is a serious matter. One of the worst occurred in 1783. On that occasion 14,000 persons were killed. In the eruption of 1875, the vegetation, which provided for 40,000 sheep, 2,000 cattle, and 3,000 horses, was all destroyed. The hay harvest, the only one in Iceland, was also entirely destroyed. Scoriæ, varying from fine pumice to pieces the size of two fists, covered its surface from an inch and a half to eight inches deep. The eruption began about nine A.M., and when the scoriæ fell there was total darkness. The air was so highly charged with electricity that staff-spikes held up in the hand seemed to be in a blaze.

We soon began to descend a little to a vast plateau. Our provisions had been fallen back upon every few hours, and were now much reduced. The farmer looked forward to the plateau as being likely to afford some *multeber*, a kind of raspberry with a hard skin, but juicy. A good and most useful man was the farmer. Favoured by the weather, he steered well, and we soon came to an incline on the snow, where we could make a long and safe *glissade*. It was certainly a novelty to see us all flying down. The farmer was the best man, and happily we reached the bottom in safety. Another hour and we lay down to rest and enjoy our *multeber*. They were deliciously refreshing. The house-painter, or *maler*, suggested that there was a *sæter* somewhere at the head of Eikesdal which we might try for. "That is just what we are making for," said our cheery chief, the farmer; "in about an hour we shall be there." On we went, our fatigue being forgotten in the grandeur of the scenery and the difficulty of picking one's way, for hopping from stone to stone absorbs the attention considerably. The time soon passed, and after we had completed our twelve hours' walk we had arrived at some weather-worn, storm-riven, dwarfed, gnarled, and twisted birches, beyond which, in a *botten*, lay our *sæter*. What an invasion! The two girls were astonished, but when they heard the voice of the farmer all was well. Ole immediately ordered a *bunker*, as it is called in Romsdal; in Gudbransdalen it is termed *rummer coller*. How we enjoyed our rest after this simple food! A *bunker*, however, should be described: it is a flat wooden tub of curds and whey, and is handed to two people. Each person is armed with a spoon, with which it is etiquette to draw a line across the centre for your *vis-à-vis* to eat up to, not beyond; but few Englishmen ever reach the line unless they are very old hands.

We were now at the head of the Eikesdal gorge, or valley; a roaring

Rob Hooker.

torrent rushed down the centre to Utigaard; on the left were steep precipices with a large fall; while the opposite side was perpendicular, and threatened showers of troll stones. As we descended we saw many huge masses of rocks which had ploughed their way down, carrying all before them. To see one of these *lapsus naturæ* is a very impressive sight, and makes one hold his breath and think. Passing through the valley, we noticed some very curious snow shoes, in form like the square frames on which sea-lines are wound, but with broader cross-pieces. Birch twigs on each side and over the foot fix them. On we trudged, having bidden farewell to the farmer, thanked him for his good services, and had a *skaal* for Gamle Norge. Finally, we left the house-painter at his destination, where the old lady told us all about the dust coming down upon her; and then Ole and myself were alone to finish the day. We had started at four A.M., and it was now ten P.M. We at length saw the spire of a church—the kirk at Utigaard—and we began to inquire for Torstin Utigaard of Utigaard, the hunter. At last we found his house, but he was on the fjeld. Could we get a bed anywhere? No, nothing. Ole persevered, and we presently found comfort. Torstin was expected down from the fjeld that night with an English gentleman, whose servant most kindly gave me his bed. After awhile down they came. Enter Torstin, a grand-looking fellow, drenched. They had killed a *semle ku*, and had left two men behind to bring it down next day. In the morning they arrived with it, forming the wildest reunion of hunters. The Finmark dog, quite black, looked a beauty as he lay by the dead reindeer. "Blenk"—for such was his name—was a good and trusty servant: neither biped nor quadruped would venture to interfere with him when he was on duty. It was a splendid group, worthy of the pencil of a Landseer.

After the pouring rain of the previous evening, which had continued through the night, we all had hopes of fine weather for our trip, and still more did we desire to see, before leaving, Utigaard in the beauty of sunshine. But no; on arising at about five, we found dirtier weather than ever; the mist low down; Blenk still keeping watch by the reindeer which had been brought down; every kind of waterproof oilskin being looked out; and a great demand for sou'-westers. At last the *stolkjær* was packed, and everything ready to go down to the boats. The baggage on the *stolkjær* was surmounted by a reindeer head, Blenk ever in attendance, and Torstin Utigaard of Utigaard leading the pony as our chief. Then we were off, looking something between fishermen and smugglers.

It was with much regret we took our last look at Utigaard as we settled down in the boats *en route* for Syltebø. The valley was grand in the extreme, the mist sometimes breaking up over the sky-line with a sudden rush, as if thankful to get loose and range over the fjeld with freedom. Hardly were we under way, and the crew settled down to the steady-going pace which Norwegians can keep up for any length of time, when Utigaard burst out wondering who could have been the figures he telescoped on the snow on the previous day—the fellows who had nearly spoilt their sport and frightened their deer at the very moment when they thought they had the "rein" well in hand. What could people be doing up there? why should they go? who had ever seen any one in that part of the fjeld? At last the thought flashed across his mind that it might have been us. Was it? Yes, most undoubtedly it was, but happily we had unintentionally turned the deer; it was, however, the right way, so no harm had been done.   The deer had been bagged, and we now all rejoiced together.

As the three boats rowed steadily in solemn procession down the *vand* we approached the Vika Pass on the starboard side.   At this point the

Eikesdal.

lake is most imposing, its grandeur much enhanced by the mist, which is ever changing, ever beautiful in form and intensity.   Soon some of the favourite old Norwegian songs were started, the chorus being echoed by the other boats.   On the opposite side of the Vika Pass there had been a great *steen-skred;* and so immense are the surroundings that it was

I olât.

impossible to realise the extent of the devastation until we approached the base of it, as it had dashed and lumbered into the lake; then the huge masses revealed themselves in their unmistakable proportions, dwarfing our boats to mere insignificant specks by their side.

Near this spot bears have been seen, and one was tracked only lately. This led to the subject of bear-traps and "self-shooters," when the Tentmaster-general enlarged on the *modus operandi* adopted by the postmaster at Sundal. He knew there were bears, and having fully studied the spot, determined to lay a "self-shooter," if possible, or at all events a trap; and this he very ingeniously so arranged that when the trap caught Master Bruin a red flag should go up: this he could see with a telescope from the post-office as he sat sorting the letters. Some people had noticed that the latter operation took much longer than usual about this time; still no one attributed the delay to the post-master's love of bear-hunting, and they little thought that he sorted with one eye and watched for Bruin with the other. At last one day the postmaster saw the red flag. This was too much; the letter eye immediately joined the fun. He was off at once to the bear, shot him, and brought him home; and during the year he managed to get four.

Hard as it rained, we were very sorry when our boat trip drew to a close, and we felt that we should soon have to bid farewell to Torstin and Eikesdal Lake, with its many joys, rough life, and hearty welcomes. We had a glorious walk from the lake to Syltebø, and were glad when we saw in the distance the white house which was to be our haven of rest, and to welcome us as friends. Soon after our arrival our host came in from the river with a good fish; and many a one has been taken from that stream, in spite of the change which has come over Norwegian rivers within the last few years. When English sportsmen began fishing in Norway the *bønder* attached no value to salmon. They were surprised to see them caught with such slight rods and tackle; but, as soon as it dawned upon them that salmon were worth so much per pound, they began to help themselves by netting them at the mouth of the river, before they could ascend the stream which the enthusiastic Piscator had

paid a good sum to rent.   The natural consequence is that Norwegian
rivers do not afford the sport they once did.

Whilst shooting at Syltebø, one of my friends found a beautiful
specimen of amethystic crystal of considerable size.   From here a steamer
runs to Molde, one of the northern sea-coast centres, and true to its time
the little screw came off the landing-place with hardly any one on
board, for the season was far advanced: most tourists and sportsmen had
returned, and we enjoyed it all the more, as it afforded us a better opportunity of seeing the people themselves.

The variety in Norwegian travel adds greatly to one's enjoyment.
In the present trip we started from a rich expansive valley; thence we
ascended through woods of birch and alder by a torrent's side, vegetation
became stunted and sparse, mosses gradually disappeared, and lichens
preponderated; then came barren boulders, and, above all, the everlasting
snow.   Having attained this, our journey was varied by a descent to
the wild gorge of Utigaard; the Lake of Eikesdal, a vast body of water,
with its grand fall; then again, after the boating procession, through
the valley of Syltebø, by the side of its salmon river, to the sea; and
finally we were on the deck of the bustling little screw steamer.   On
stopping at the first place we were surprised to see a large boat coming
off, mushroomed with huge umbrellas, whence issued the music of Norwegian voices, and evidently those of ladies; but as they neared the
steamer the soft strains ceased, and they came alongside in silence.   Our
array of oilskins, waterproofs, and sou'-westers announced that foreigners
were on board.   We, however, considered that this treasure trove should
not be a dead letter on a rainy day, and the Patriarch broached the
subject of Norwegian music, which happily led to an encore of all the
boat songs and many others, reinforced with much gusto by the chorus
of oilskins, waterproofs, and sou'-westers.   They were a happy band—all
ladies and no gentlemen—going to a party at the *præstegaard*, some few
miles down the fjord.   They assured us the priest would be very pleased
to see us, and give us a hearty welcome.   It was with much regret we
were compelled to decline the invitation, especially as it would have
afforded a pleasing episode in our trip, and given us an opportunity of

Syltelç: with Farm Implements.

seeing the *vie intime* of a Norwegian minister's home *en fête*. As their boat left the steamer, they sang one of our favourite songs, and our modest chorus followed it at a gradually increasing distance until both faded away. After this cheerful but soaking morning we comforted ourselves with stories of the fjeld, salmon, and Norwegian life. Happily the Tent-master-general was in great force, and, when called upon for a yarn, responded with "muckle hilarity," giving us one of his reindeer experiences. Can we do better than repeat it here?

First scene, *tente abri* on the fjeld. Snow close above; in fact, too much snow for sport. The Tentmaster-general telescoping alone in the camp, if one may so call two tents. Having had a very hard and weary stalk on the previous day, he was resting whilst the Major and Dan went up after deer. Soon after they had settled down to work, the Finmark dog "Passop" became very uneasy, and so fretted the string by which he was led that Dan thought he might break away, which would be sudden destruction to everything; he therefore carried the dog in his arms. Shortly afterwards, Dan, doubtlessly becoming slightly tired of carrying the dog, relaxed his hold a little. At that moment Passop caught sight of a buck, sprang from Dan's arms, and bolted after the deer. Dan threw up his arms in despair, and gave vent to several Norwegian hunting quotations unfavourable to Passop's future happiness. One thing was certain—the dog would go till he died from sheer exhaustion, and Dan would never recover his favourite Finmarker. Dan soliloquised, and watched long with his telescope, and finally gave way to grief. The next few hours were very blank and sad—deer and Passop both gone. In the afternoon, with melancholy thoughts and sluggish conversation, they began retracing their steps to the camp, which was about six miles distant. As soon as they were in sight of their fjeld home the Tentmaster-general came cheerfully to meet them, for he had seen seven deer steadily going down to a lake, and had anxiously awaited the return of Passop. No time, however, was to be lost. Off he went in pursuit alone, with the Major's rifle. Hardly had he got away from the camp when he caught a glimpse of more deer—two this time, both going to the edge. He lay down to watch them, for patience as well as judg-

ment is required in reindeer work. After some time a strange sound,
like the bark of a dog, came down; but who ever heard the bark of a
dog in the wilds of the fjeld and on the snow? Listening again, in a
few minutes, from behind a huge boulder, came a *stor buck* straight on,
with a dog close behind. What a chance! Happily the Tentmaster was
equal to the occasion. In the twinkling of an eye the shot was fired, the
buck was hit, but carried his bullet with him, and made for the water.
The dog gaining on him a little, he dashed into the water to swim for
it; but Passop dashed in too, for by this time our hunter had recovered
from his astonishment at the strange dog, and recognised it as Passop.
The ice-water of these lakes is, of course, intensely cold, and the dog
was obliged to come back: he, however, did not do so until he had had
a good tug at the deer, which by this time had turned on his side and
was dead. A second time Passop tried to reach him, and was obliged
to return; but the third time he got on his back, and sitting there, held
the horns in his teeth. As the dog could not bring him ashore, what was
to be done? By this time the Major had come up, and determined to swim
for him, and tow him on shore. The ice-water was too cold for him also,
and he was obliged to turn back. The deer was too far out to lasso, even
could they lead the line up from the camp. But *nil desperandum.* Hardly
had their wondering got full swing when a tremendous squall swept down
the hillside, caught the deer and Passop, and they drifted in. The Major
made another attempt, and the deer was landed. They were soon off to
the camp, where Dan, with a very sad heart, was preparing *speise.* When
the latter looked up and saw them coming, accompanied by his beloved
dog, his expression soon changed, and Passop was caught up into his
arms as quickly as he had sprung from them in the morning, while Dan,
with a radiant face and his head a little on one side, turning round to the
Tentmaster-general, said, "Good man, Maget good man." Passop was
made much of, Dan's happiness restored, and the one bottle of champagne
was iced in the snow, to drink to "Rensdyr jagt paa hoie fjeld." It was a
great day happily terminated, and long to be remembered.

FOR some days we had been on the tramp, and arrived at Indfjord. Thursday, August 20th, 1875, was a sad day there. Returned from a long tour though very wild, rough districts, where neither food nor lodgings were to be had, we were settling down for a good night's rest, certainly under difficulties, at the house of a good farmer named Ole Erikson Boe, when the gruesome news came of a disaster in the mountains above. A tremendous rock crash, or *steen-skred*, had taken place at a spot called Sylbotten, some three thousand feet above, where there were two *sæters* occupied by two *piger*, who had charge of the cows belonging to the good people down the valley. We started off at once. In a more than quiet spot like this, with what a crash does such news burst upon every one! What sympathy it brings out; what interest in the details of the occurrence! What sadness marks each face, and how quiet and subdued all are, though all are talking!

We pass on, with a little provision in our wallets, and soon come to some reapers in the valley, working in the fields, with leather aprons for their protection. We started with Halve Jacobsen, the owner of the *sæter*, who went up, taking a pony and foal, in case the mare's services were required: the foal always runs by the mother. On our sad mission we could not be otherwise than struck with the joyfulness of this young animal, its abounding spirits, caprioles, and quirks and capers. Before arriving at the steep part of the ascent we stopped at a small outbuilding close to the farm, the front of the house looking over the Indfjord, with a grand expanse before one, the morning light shimmering down to the edge of the water far, far below, and all seeming peace and gladness. At the back of the house, between that and the *haave*, we found a vastly different scene—pain, grief, and heavy hearts. What a contrast to the brightness on the fjord side—the sunny side that was! The anxious group was in shadow, comparatively speaking, the centre attraction being a roughly made stretcher, on which was lying, hardly conscious, pale, agonized, and bone-broken, Ingeborg, Erichsdatter, Griseth. Poor girl! she had been brought down some three thousand feet by a very steep *sœter* path—for there was hardly any road—jogged and shaken, with one leg broken, ribs crushed, and her face much cut and bruised by the cracking up of the *sœter* before the overwhelming force which carried it away. Around her were the *bönder* folk, and one poor old woman whose

Looking across Indfjord.

grief seemed beyond consolation. The autumn was advanced, and the winter coming quickly on, for the first snow days had begun. She had only one cow to support her: that was at Sjolbotten, and was killed, so her only hope of livelihood was for the moment swept from her, as no cow could be got under £5, and "no siller had she." What a chance for some rich Samaritan to heal a broken heart for the small sum of £5!

But as "many a mickle makes a muckle," so, doubtless, would a new cow be bought by the kindly spirits of the good Indfjord folk. Their love for each other is a lesson to even the most civilised among us. Indeed, it is very noticeable that small communities care for everybody, while large masses notice no individual—only charitable institutions.

But we have not yet commenced the ascent. The mare leads through

The Hall at Grvolt.

the brushwood, the cheerful foal diverging now and then in the self-conceit of all young things, fancying they know better than their mothers. It was a steep climb. The mare slipped; but Halve said it was all right, she knew the way. The morning was warm, and, as soon as we arrived at a kind of ledge looking over the valley and fjord, we halted. What a lovely, or rather, what a grand scene it was! Still there was no forgetting our mission—no shaking off its sadness. Our present object, after Ingeborg's arrival. was to go up and see after her companion, Ingrana. Our halt was not for long. We had already taken off our coats, and hung them on a pine-stump. To our surprise, Halve left his there until our return, and said, when we did not, " You can leave anything as you like in Gamle Norge."

En route, in three hours we had left our last brier and alder behind, and were on the plateau of the High Fjeld, and found much *smörgrass*, so good for cows. As *smör* is the Norse for butter, it will explain the name. For a long time we tramped over the *botten*, carpeted with rich flora ; but at the end we saw the *steen-skred*, or landslip. Some four or five *bönder* were already there, and seemed very surprised to see a foreigner coming up with Halve. A few words of explanation, and all was understood : one common object in view, that of helping each other, soon bound us together. Ingrana naturally had not been to sleep since the disaster. It is difficult to imagine any Norske *pige* nervous, but poor Ingrana had been shaken and frightened out of her wits. Her description, after a little entreaty and patience on the part of the persuader, ran thus :—Early in the morning Ingrana was awakened by a heavy rolling sound of thunder, followed directly by a crash. She rushed from her *sæter*, and, coming out of her door, saw Ingeborg's *sæter* carried away and buried. It is difficult to realise the feelings of this simple-minded girl, living so solitary a life for three months. In a moment—a second of time—one was taken and the other left. Ten cows also were buried ; and, no help being at hand, Ingrana had to go down this lonely mountain with the sad news, leaving her companion fixed, pinned, and crushed until she could return with assistance

We arrived after three and a half hours' hard ascent, when some sour milk that had been left was given us. The Englishman elicited a smile from Ingrana when, taking the bowl from his lips, his moustache was white with cream. This was hopeful and a good sign.

The slip was accelerated by a very large waterspout striking the face of the mountain, as amongst the rocks which were brought down was a quantity of sand, and the presence and action of water were palpable, deep

Landslip at Sylbotten : Indfjord.

pools being left in many places. The scene was appalling—a wreck in the wildest sense of the word. Some three-quarters of a mile of mountain side had come down, carrying all before it—*rammeding*, as the Norse word is. Huge rocks, a few stunted trees, hardly any kind of herbage—what a hurly-burly of desolation! Looking across and over it, we saw the distant placid fjord and open sea. What a contrast, the peace of one and the turbulence of the other! Still the damage was a known quantity, every year something of the kind happening, sometimes with loss of life, sometimes without. The accompanying sketch was taken from the lower portion, looking upwards.

After going over the greater part of this chaos we went back to the preserved *sæter*, where we were most kindly received, our sympathy being accepted in the same spirit in which it was offered. Then we returned. We found Halve's coat quite safe and undisturbed, and after the usual time arrived at Ole Erikson Boe's farm, where we had a simple repast of good *fladbrod* and *bunker*, there being no meat here. We rested, and early in the morning started for Fiva. During the evening Boe showed me an old Danske Bible, folio size, A.D. 1590, with large brass clasps. The good folk wanted me to bring my wife to the funeral, in case the poor girl should not survive. In the morning we went down to the shore, as we heard the steamer for Molde was coming in to take Ingeborg thither, should she be still alive. Life was all but extinct when she was got on board. Ole Fiva and myself started in a boat for Veblungsnæs, having thanked the good people of Indfjord for their kind welcome, and they expressing their gratitude for our interest and sympathy, and reiterating their desire to welcome my wife at Indfjord.

The morning was lovely for boat travel; such peace that convulsions like those we had witnessed seemed incredible. But it was no dream: the inhabitants of Indfjord, the family of Ingeborg, Ingrana, and the poor woman without her solitary cow, all were stern realities.

Soon after our return to Fiva we heard that Ingeborg was dead, had been taken back from Molde, and was to be buried in the *gravsted* at Indfjord on September 2nd, 1875. Accordingly, early that morning we started in carrioles from Fiva to Veblungsnæs, where myself, wife, daughter, and Ole Fiva took a boat with six oars for Indfjord. A lovely, peaceful morning it was as we left the landing-place at Veblungsnæs. Soon the six oars began their sturdy dip as we came under the shadow of the mountains : the dip was strong, as Norwegians only can row for a long travelling sweep and perfect time. After settling down with our *line* of provisions—for we were travelling Norskily, and no Norske is complete without a well-filled *line*—a sad tone seemed pervading the boat : our mission was one of sympathy for the bereavement of others, with an after-thought of thankfulness that we had been spared in health, and were sound in body and bone. But the melancholy of every one was broken by a remark from Ole that we should soon see the Runic *steen*, which is about half a Norske mile from Veblungsnæs. A lieutenant of engineers, who was superintending a new bridge, had described this stone to us, and we were eager to see it. At last we came upon it. The boatman ran alongside, and threw water over it to develop it. In nine hundred years pluvial attrition alone is sure to make its mark, to say nothing of our energetic friend Neptune's constant storm-drift and tempest. (The writer would apologize for the term "pluvial attrition," but there are so many long words about just now, what with street advertisements and urban authors.) A general view of the Runic stone is given in the opposite engraving, while the initial ornament on page 175 was drawn from a plant plucked on the spot. The letters are thirteen in number, and their length about eighteen inches. Twelve feet from the sea-level, under low-water mark, and projecting some few feet, runs a ledge of rocks, beneath which is supposed to be secreted untold wealth.

The translation of these Runic hieroglyphics is, "The Court of Justice," and this inscription was evidently placed in a conspicuous position to guide any who came to the court in old pagan days ; for Romsdal was one of the last of the pagan strongholds. Above, high up, close to Sylbotten, was a pagan temple : but the Court of Justice was held at Devold, Romsdal.

There was now a regular good settle down for a long pull. Up to this time we have been in shadow, but now we round a point, and taking what a landsman would call the "first on the left," we go due south down to Indfjord. The sea-water is beautifully clear, reflecting the quartz rocks, a metroll, like the good old chandeliers of our grandfathers after a spring

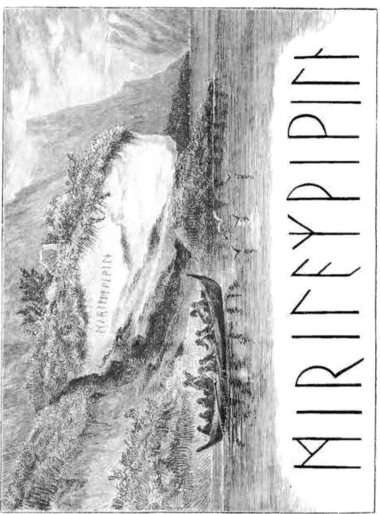

Runic Stone, with Inscription, near Indsjord.

cleaning; the rich sunlit yellow seaweed is grander far than ormolu; and here are three herons in repose, water-ousels with their snow-white breasts, and now and then sparkles by an old cormorant or diver. As we go down the fjord the snow range at the end of it blocks in everything, the morning mist waiting in the valley for exit, if possible.

By this time we near the hamlet, and high above us on the left, on a kind of plateau, we see many figures congregated. They were in front of Erich's house, Griseth being the name of the farm. We soon steered in, and then between two boathouses, at a rude pile-driven landing-place, the well-known scrape of keel on shore was heard, and we had safely arrived at Indfjord. Griseth had sent down to meet us and invite us up to the house, but we return the message that we would rather not disturb the family, but await their arrival at the *gravsted;* so, with our *line*, we picked out a spot for lunch, and enjoyed some cold reindeer meat, biscuit, cheese, &c. During lunch we could see the *bönder* folk collecting high up at Griseth, overlooking the fjord, and at two o'clock we saw them by the telescope start down the narrow mountain path, the coffin being lashed on to the little cart to prevent it slipping. Soon they were lost in a dip of the wood, from which they emerged nearer to us. As we stood at the *gravsted*, or grave-place—like our word homestead, home-place—a man came up and shook hands with us, and then standing on the wall, commenced tolling the bell; for there is no church, but only a bell-tower.

Soon the procession drew near. First came the coffin, black, lashed on to the hay-cart, and drawn by a beautiful young *blakken*, or Norske pony, whose collar was of old carved wood painted, the *bonde* driver walking behind the coffin, which bore three wreaths of wild flowers. At a distance behind the coffin followed the men, and after an interval the sorrowing women, who were succeeded by men of the family, many sad hearts, and Ingrana. It was a modest but impressive scene. When the pony arrived at the *gravsted*, hearing the tolling bell, he shied and jibbed, as if regretting what he had done. The coffin was therefore carried in at once. There being no clergyman, a friend sang a hymn. The coffin was lowered into the grave; the wreaths removed; the ropes withdrawn. Some one said to Ingrana, " You were lucky to escape." " I could not have been

ready," she said ; " God wanted me not, and left me a little longer. She
was ready," meaning Ingeborg, whom they were burying. They then
sang the second hymn, " Hjemme, Hjemme," as the friends shovelled the
earth in, and the heavy thud of the large spadeful boomed like parts of
Handel's " Dead March " in *Saul*. After filling in the grave the wreaths
were placed on the newly raised mound, and the ceremony closed with
" Hjemme." The weird sea birds screamed, and all went away together.
Many will recount the story of Ingeborg, Erichsdatter, Griseth.

Before leaving the *gravsted* the grave-boards must be noted, they being
so remarkable in form, so quaint, and also so Bosphoric. Sometimes a
white butterfly is introduced, as typical of the soul. How different from
the present association with the allegory of their transient nothingness !
After the funeral we had to pay two or three visits. All the farmers wanted
us to visit them—some to tell of sport, others to offer us *aqua vitæ* and
stamped cakes like the Dutch *waffles ;* and when we returned to Ole Erikson
Boe's he gave me an old Norske belt as a memento of our visit, which we
need hardly say is most carefully treasured.

So passed away Ingeborg, Erichsdatter of Griseth, while Ingrana
remained waiting her bidding.

STERDAL is full of interest and character, with a wild
river, precipitous mountains on either side, snow on
the high peaks above, a rushing of waters below,
hardly any track, and shut in by a façade of rock at
the end of the valley ; and yet it is the way from
Romsdal to Valdal. Let us, therefore, explore it,
and do so in two fyttes—a short carriole ride to the
sætr with the ladies, and beyond, high, high up, for
real research without the ladies.

Place aux dames. We tried the short journey with two carrioles, and
for an English mile or two we did pretty well, as they will go anywhere and
over anything ; but as we got into the scrubwood and underwood the road
grew worse, the wheels going sometimes over a boulder one or two feet in
height, the axle assuming an alarming angle, and the *skyd-gut* hanging on

The Gravestead: Ingeborg's Funeral, Balljord.

the high side to keep the vehicle from turning over —first one side and then the other—till the fair occupants of the machine were shaken to a jelly, and would fain try to walk. Still we all persevere, and soon arrive at the meal-mill, given in the accompanying page illustration. What a retired spot for business! Who would ever think of it as a centre to draw customers and found a business—as a likely spot for a man beginning with the conventional half-crown becoming the architect of his own fortune?

The water seen here is the Ister—ever thick and muddy, and always in violent motion. What a contrast to the calm dignity of the adjacent mountains in all their graduated phases! A little above this is a shoot which brings down water to turn the mill. On our arrival the miller comes out with a quiet kind of welcome, and very kindly shows us the stones doing their share of work to bring about *fladbrod* for the people of the valley during their summer visit: it is for the *sæter* people they work principally.

Leaving the mill, we pass on to the denser scrub and brushwood. We had with us an old Skye terrier, full of noble traits of character—courage and endurance—but being as blind as Belisarius, and running against some of the rocks in the track, he was not only thrown on his haunches, but his nerve was shaken—that Highland nerve which is of such rare stuff. Let us immortalise our blind Norwegian canine traveller by a description. If lost, an advertisement should run thus:— "Lost, a brindled Skye terrier, answering to the name of 'Kyle.' Rough broken hair, broad chest, short-legged, bow-legged, middle-aged and strong, and carries his tail high. True to the core, with a head as large as a deerhound's. Teeth to match." The Norwegians at first thought it would be well to shoot him, but when they came to know him better he soon enlisted them all among his many ardent admirers.

Perhaps the idea may flit across the mind of some, Why bring a blind Scotch terrier into a work on Norway? This is why: old Kyle was taken that day for a young bear by a simple-minded Norwegian cow. Never were fear and fright more vividly portrayed than by the action of that animal, and of her tail especially, on the first glimpse of the brown brindled terrier. Hearing his name mentioned, he has just wagged his

tail, which is quite flat, like an otter's, and when very pleased he wags it
with the flat side on to the floor to produce more sound.

By this time we are at the *sæter*, where the *piger* have come to look
after the cows until September. Having driven on to the only flat piece
of grass, we unpack for lunch, when the produce of the aforesaid cows
comes to our comfort in an unadulterated form, and thoroughly is the
simple fare enjoyed. After lunch we visit the interior of the *sæter*, and
find spinning going on steadily, a little national tune being hummed to

Spinning in the Sæter, Isterdal.

the whirring wheel accompaniment. The weaving is done during the
winter months. In the summer a little spinning is done, but only by the
most industrious.

To see Isterdal the only way is to walk. Let us, therefore, continue
on from the *sæter* in the direction of the Valdal. This was done with Ole
Fiva. Soon we began to ascend, for the end of the valley is precipitous,
with a fine fall, the top of which must be reached before arriving at the
plateau, *botten*, or *bolloch*. On commencing the ascent Ole pointed out
in the river below a spot where a bear had been killed; and higher up

The Head of the Valley: Isterdal.

again where a bear lived, for he had seen it there. Some idea of the situation is given by the opposite woodcut, with the *aiguilles* on the right. This is looking down Isterdal. The path was effaced the day before we passed by the descent of a quantity of rough stuff, more than sufficient to have carried us with it into the valley beneath. The *aiguilles* are of a similar formation to the Troltinderne in Romsdal, and seem to be a nursery of trolds for future ages.

The evening glows on these pinnacles are marvellously and beautifully grand, and the transitions of hue from one to the other beyond imagination and conception. Still we work up. Ole, ignoring the slightly defined regular track, goes up really awful places, hauling himself up, and astonishing his follower and companion by displaying the most unnecessary and enviable agility. All honour to such strength and energy! By this time we had reached the plateau from which the murky Ister takes a header into the valley which lay at our feet. Once on the plateau, we could get along better over the stunted flora and bare rocks, with snow here and there, especially on the south-west side. The track is indicated by a few pieces of rock, put here and there in a pile, which being of the same formation as the rock we are walking on, the similarity of colour makes them very indistinct at times: the best way is to look out for one on the sky-line, if possible. After a long tramp we crossed the Ister again, and found it still more turbid, which was puzzling, as it seemed to come from a glacier above; but of this more anon. We worked on until we could look down Valdal, and having drunk in nature in that direction, took a little food from our wallets, and lay down for an *al fresco* siesta on a handsome natural carpet of *fjelde reis* and other vegetation.

After that, Ole began telling of expeditions, traditions, and excursions to the Jager's Steen, and formally wound up with the report of a frozen lake which a hunter had seen, but which had not been visited since. Could we find it? Was the Herr inclined to go? "Most certainly." So we started.

There is a wonderful sense of freedom, and yet of a closer commune with one's Creator, in wandering over almost untrodden ground to admire some portion of his works that have been rarely visited by man. It is suggestive of drawing aside the veil of the tabernacle of nature; and happy is the man who derives comfort and soul strength in so doing! Ole led straight up over rocks bare and betumbled; not a symptom of vegetation; above us a glacier coming to the edge of a precipice, and the melting ice forming a fringed fall. We lay down, looking over the side on a bed of scarlet and crimson *fjeld-ris*, a kind of cotoneaster. Beyond this ledge we saw the glacier imperceptibly coming on, backed in the long perspective

Melting Glacier over Valdal.

of glacial blocks by a huge bare mass of rock, the Biskop, and the Dronningen. This was the source of the Ister. The water, some distance from the foot of the fall, passed over a soft deposit, which sullied its pristine purity right down to the sea, the "murky Ister," thus acquiring near its origin its characteristic turbidity.

Now for a try for the unknown lake. Ole keeps on, thinking he has his bearings all right. At last, having climbed up by the side of a fall dashing down through bare rocks, came the summit, and creeping round a boulder, before us lies a lake intensely deep in colour, and full of icebergs and floes of old ice. Where we stood there was snow, with tracks of reindeer; but in places the former had melted, the *lemmings* had been there, and the reindeer-flowers were coming up. These we eat with *fladbrød og smør* after a time, for we could not at once settle down to a snack without paying a tribute of respect to the majesty of nature before us. Beginning our meal in earnest, in the midst of it we heard a noise like a roll of thunder, the direction of which we soon discovered. On the left side of the lake the vast expanse of snow was riven by a gigantic avalanche, which ploughed its way down, and, coming to the edge of the rocks, plunged headlong into the lake, agitating all the ice, and causing the icebergs to jostle each other; but both water and ice soon regained their equilibrium, and nature lay before us in solemn silence and undisturbed majesty. It can well be imagined that having once attained such a spot—some 5,000 feet above the sea—there was a desire to linger, though the day was fading, and we had five and a half hours' walk home. However, " En route ! " was the word. Straight down from bare rock to rock simply ends in no knees after a time, and one's legs become something between strips of asparagus and sea-kale. There was, however, one thing in store : once on a fair road, we could make some running. It was a lovely evening: we were late, it was true, but, as horses go freely with their noses towards home, we both took to the road very kindly, and went along with a will. Ole did not talk much. It is the pace that kills, and after sixteen hours' trudge with our provisions, he no doubt felt that he had done enough. With health and strength, such a day amidst grand scenery is a joy for ever.

Church Axe.

CEREMONIES, WEDDINGS, ETC.

CEREMONIES, WEDDINGS, ETC.

 N all climes and in all stages of civilisation a wedding
is an object of special interest, and is likely to bring
forward some traits of national character. The bride
is always the great attraction, of course, whether
plain or old—not that any bride should ever be plain,
however uncomely featured she may be, for on that
day of all others, the spirit should shine through the
clay, with every hope of happiness before her; and if
there be happiness in the world, surely it must be when the bride
becomes the better-half of him she loves. Let us, then, attend a Norske
wedding.

Weddings are not now as they used to be in the "good old days,"
when knives and winding-sheets were a part of the programme—when grim
rehearsals of the "Grapplers" were frequently repeated, and two com-
batants, with one belt round the two waists, grappled and struck until one
was vanquished. No; Scandinavian ferocity is subsiding; they think more
now of "bleeding" their foreign visitors, and the weddings are sobered
down; but the arch-fiend of inebriation tightens his grip, and Norwegian
weddings in the provinces are characterized by deep libations and their
wretched consequences. Now, having noticed the worst feature of these
Northern domestic gatherings, let us turn cheerily to the brighter side of
them.

Naturally costume immensely assists a ceremony like this, and should the bride not have old silver enough of her own, everybody is ready to contribute towards the general result, and is only too glad to do anything in his power to add to the brightness of the occasion. In Norway the bride wears a silver crown, which varies a little in form according to date, the most modern crowns branching out all round more than the older ones. The silver crowns are generally made with hinges, four or six in number, so that they may fold up into a small space for carrying in a *tine*, or box. The oldest forms are silver-gilt; the more recent are partially gilt, some

parts being left bright silver. The bride also wears a thick curb chain, with a medal, which is sometimes set in filigree-work; but in the case under notice the medal was one cast with a fine bust of Nelson. Tidemand, the Norwegian genre painter, has portrayed many scenes of the "Bride preparing to start," "Dressing the Bride," &c.

The procession to the church is generally all-important. First comes the fiddler, next the *kander* or tankard man, then best man, bride and bridegroom, fathers, mothers, sisters, brothers, friends, relations, and many others—all the children of the place swarming round the church door. We should observe that there is a stolid immobility about some of the Norwegian *piger* which seems to become intensified on these occasions; but when they do melt there must be a great overflow of spirit and reaction.

The picturesque group at the altar of the church takes one back to the Middle Ages: the bride resplendent in costume—in some cases quaint to a degree, especially in Sætersdalen—with the old silver brooches, rings, and pendants of generations long gathered to their fathers; the bridegroom also, most likely, in costume, with his best man close by to look after the bridesmaid; in the centre, the Elizabethan ruff, pure white as in Queen Elizabeth's time, thrown vigorously up by the sombre black gown, renders the priest a prominent figure; while perhaps a ray from the sun, descending on the group, shines upon the bride at the very moment when that ray only

A Bridal Party crossing the Fjord.

is wanted to complete the pictorial effect of the grouping and its surroundings. The verger, or clerk, with his long red pole—the functionary described in a former chapter—is not on active service to-day to awake the sleepers; in fact, the congregation seems rather inclined to turn the tables and wake him up. The church floor is, as usual, strewn with juniper tips, and after the ceremony the bride and bridegroom start home. Walk, ride, drive, or boat—that depends on the distance and character of the road to be traversed. They are all picturesque: the water, however, carries the palm, and, as we have before remarked, the whole scene causes one to

The Wedding.

revert to early days, before carriages were used, or roads were uninviting for travel, and when locomotion was a difficulty.

What an evening it was, "the bride's return!" As usual in Norway, you cannot go far without crossing a fjord: this the bride had to do. A twenty-oared sea-boat was her water carriage. What peace—what colour— what harmony! Was it typical of her future married life? A zephyr just filled the broad sail, the large prow rearing grandly in front, with a huge bunch of flowers and green things innumerable on the top; then a large flag and more flowers at the mast-head; and the rowers every now and then bursting out into a refrain, which as one leaves off the other takes up.

And how these Norsemen do row—always together! It is generally allowed, by men of experience in Norway, that so long as the rower is not too "arch-fiended" to sit up, he will always keep time with his oar. The dip of the oars in the calm is delightfully refreshing, and the regular sweep gives an idea of power. Fun is going on at the other end of the boat; for

Drinking Horn in the Collection of C. Hampden Wigram, Esq.

the bride is there on a raised seat, with the bridegroom, supported by their friends. The second boat is being left behind, so the *kander-man* is holding a large silver tankard to encourage and at the same time joke them. Doubtless a spurt will be put on after this, and another race commenced for the run home; or they may just stop for one more *skaal* (the bride's

health), and when they have once commenced, be undecided as to going home.

One thing is a comfort, at all events: all through the country there is strong evidence of family affection, and these weddings are only the beginning of a new era of happiness. In Thelemarken, as we have already

The Bride's Return by Water.

had occasion to remark, one custom is for the bridegroom to elaborately carve the *stabur*, or family treasure-house, with excellent designs and cunning work, which he effects with his tolle-knife; and another is to carve good mottoes on the large beds and over the doors of the rooms. The following are some from Thelemarken district, that quaint land of short waists, shoulder-blades, and white jackets—a land abounding with grand old conscientious work; huge timbers made into solid houses; no hurry-skurry, no slurriness, no giving as little as possible for wages received—real good timber-work; while inside may be found carved chests, some of them family treasures handed down for generations. Motto over bed, carved in: "This is my bed and resting-place, where God gives me peace and rest, that I may healthy arise and serve Him." Over the entrance to a house: "Stand, house, in the presence of our Lord, assured from all danger, from fire and theft. Save it, thou, O God; bless also all who go in and all who go out here." The ale-bowls, too, have good mottoes: "Of me you must drink; but swear not, nor ever drink too much." This motto we would recommend to the licensed victuallers of England, as good for their "pewters." Another drinking-bowl: "I am as a star unto you, and all the girls drink of me willingly." Another: "Taste of the fruit of the corn-field, and thank God from your inmost heart." This one again: "Drink me forthwith, and be thankful, for I shall soon be no more." These, we say, are good sentiments, and worthy of note; and they must be the outcome of deeply rooted honest hearts, anxious to benefit not only those about them, but those who may follow.

When the bride returns home there are great doings, with firing of guns, and, as we have before observed, libations and dancing; the latter doing good and giving pleasure, the former, to say the least of them, producing the next day what is known in Scotland as the "blacksmith's hammer on the forehead."

What a contrast to a Norwegian wedding, carried out with all its details, is the modern civilisation of being married before a "Registrar"—a process which must be sudden death to sentiment, and destructive of all the sacred associations so closely linked with the solemnity of marriage in Norway! Marriage takes time. The Lutheran Church has two distinct services or

ceremonies, which conduce to the steady-going of the young people
concerned, and tend to develop prudent and careful living.   There is first
the betrothal, and then the wedding.   Circumstances decide the particular
period between the two events—one year generally, sometimes two or more;
in any case the betrothal is a good preparation for the responsibilities of
married life, and certainly works well.   One thing is beyond denial—it

Before the Wedding.

affords an opportunity to discover latent objections and bad habits, which
might not crop out all at once while the lover is offering a concentrated
essence of courtship.   By the betrothal system a girl enters upon a certain
and marked position, being as it were an aspirant to the honour and dignity
of marriage; and this training has generally a most wholesome effect.
The same system is likewise carried out by the provincial peasants, though

these simple folk are sometimes a little impatient of the second ceremony; but the law of Norway has alleviated any difficulty which might arise from such impetuosity, and taken the same *status* as that of Scotland.

The wedding festival will frequently last a week—early and late. It is not " What a day we are having ! " but " What a week we are having ! " The home love of the people is prominently shown on occasions like these; their simple affection and general kindliness can only be the outcome of tenderness and sympathy in their every-day life, when the mothers are so motherly, the fathers so fatherly. No " iceberg dads " are to be found in

The Arrival at Home.

Norway; they are more like the stoves which every one gathers round for comfort when the chills of life are likely to be forthcoming. And the priest comes out strongly on these occasions, for, as we have previously noticed, he is a part of every family; he shares the troubles of the flocks, and enhances their joys. He is no kill-joy; on the contrary, he enters into all that is going on, joins in the songs, is generally convivial at table, and is not shy of tobacco; he is, in fact, a practical, genial Christian, and consequently does good service to the cause he represents and to his flock.

We now come to the last ceremonies of the Church, only remarking on our way the very great importance attached by the Lutheran Church to confirmation. In this the Church does well, and sows good seed at the

Hitterdal Church.

right time—seed which is to be the joy of riper years and the backbone of posterity.

A Norwegian funeral is surrounded by an unwholesome atmosphere of intense melancholy; hope and faith seem trampled down for the moment by the weight of present grief. The Norwegians certainly do not look upon

Return from the Christening.

the arrival of the reaper who puts in the sickle as the "order of release" from the trammels of our lower state. Perhaps their intensity of feeling is

The Funeral: Bogou.

a certain relief from which they rebound to a lighter burden in after-life. Their quiet, secluded life encourages this; the very sombreness of the country develops it; and the almost oppressive grandeur of the scenery sustains it; while the absence of birds with joyous song certainly adds to it.

Funerals in this country take many forms. First, in towns, for plump, portly burghers, as well as for men of note in letters, politics, or art, there is the old form of coffin chariot, with cock-hatted driver, the horses clothed in all the panoply of funereal darkness, the road sprinkled with juniper or yew twigs, the Death's head blended with a flame rising from the urn as decoration; the latter the only cheerful, hopeful thought in the whole

The Stolkjer and Boat.

arrangement. We regret to add that, like weddings, funerals are characterized by heavy libations. As to military obsequies, they are much the same in all lands, and therefore we need say nothing concerning them. And now, away from towns and cemeteries, to the more simple method of taking farewell of passing spirits and lifeless clay.

During the visit to Indfjord a description was given of the funeral of Ingeborg, a good *pige* swept away by a landslip. How full of sympathy the good folk were; how the finest breed of *blakken* was brought, with the best carved collar the district could produce, to honour her last remains!

This is "only one."

And in another place we referred to the more common occurrence of the coffin being placed on a *stolkjær*. During the winter, in some of the most inaccessible farms, such as the Geiranger, where there is no landing-place, the body is kept until spring. This seems protracted agony; but there is the balance of nature—no decomposition. In the less-frequented rivers a solitary boat may sometimes be seen, containing a funeral party unattended, their sorrow self-contained and unshared by others. The opposite woodcut illustrates a touching incident—a *bonde* and wife taking their "only one" to God's acre. This is secluded life intensified. Their little one—their treasure and delight, their pet lamb—was called home, and they had to take it to its resting-place. The poor mother may have borne up bravely; but the sight of the churchyard in the distance was too much for her, and at last she gave way and sobbed over the coffin. But when she arrives the priest with kindly voice and deep sympathy will comfort and cheer her. Little, however, will they talk as they row back, with their hearts full and their home empty. None but those who have had an only one called away can realise the blank—their "sunbeam" gone. The grave-boards bear simple and pious inscriptions. We append a few here.

LINES ON GRAVE-BOARDS.

TRANSLATED WORD FOR WORD FROM THE ORIGINALS.

ELI. OLSDATTER HOEL.

I was old and weary of my days, and my last footsteps were heavy; but thanks be to Jesus for his mercy, He opened my eyes so that I saw danger was near. In much trouble I must sing. Jesus is always present, and does not take his hand from us. At last I found the well from which my comfort ran.

INGRID LEDINGSÖIEN.

To children and friends! is Jesus Christ's cry: Come, see I come; mourn therefore but with hope.

Farewell. I depart. The sorrow you now taste must in love take place. God himself will guard you so that we shall soon without complaint meet before his throne.

OLE GRÖDAL.

To my Father I go home; there is rest and quiet; and I know for certain there is also a dwelling there for me prepared. Hear my sigh, Lord, and keep my spirit in thine hand.

OLE. WINNEVOLD.

Away from the world I fly full of trouble home to rest. I am ready to travel when my sweet Jesus will.

GUNDER GRÖDAL.

Seven times ten and four years was the goal the Good God had decided for us in our journey home; our mutual mother is earth. There, in the silent home of the grave, ends our last journey. Farewell then, friends, far and near. I wish every one in particular a good end.

LÖKEN.

Through pain Life is born; below the cross sin dies.
After the cross, the crown is given;
After wailing, the cry of victory.

INDRE LÖKEN.

Now have I triumphed by the blood of the wounds of Jesus. I have found my God, and gladly go to heaven.

The home life of Norway is very simple throughout: in summer, the perfect enjoyment of the short but bright season; in winter, spinning, weaving, and sledging. The absence of rudeness—the modern term "chaff" is unknown—the "even-manneredness" of the people in all classes, must strike a stranger. Whatever may be the class of society, there is always the same kindly politeness. No double set of manners, as civilisation brings about; no rudeness to inferiors, or fawning to superiors; the equal distribution of this world's goods, combined with innate kindliness, prevents this. No unkindness, for they are tender to all dumb animals, and that is an undoubted sign of sterling worth. And yet, with all this, what jolly little things the children and young folk are! They will make the most charming little curtsey, and then go off, children to the core. A good innocent romp, how they enjoy it! The young girls, too, are so natural, perfectly easy, and well behaved, that it is refreshing to be with them. Nothing prim or starched about them, but good hearts, with the bloom of youth. Their dances, too, how they enjoy them; and then a song, with a chorus from the whole company, and another dance! Capital housewives these Scandinavian maidens should make, for even the *fröken*, or young girl of position, carries out all the household duties of home, and enters into the real work of life with the greatest earnestness, being mistress of every detail, and yet the most charming of God's work—a natural lady. N.B.—The Patriarch did not lose his heart in Gamle Norge; that was safely at home in the good care of one who has monopolized it ever since he was a boy.

Norwegian housekeeping is so totally different from anything we have that it will be well to note it here. The wife has greater responsibility and requires more forethought than with us. There are no co-operative stores

Sledging.

to which to send a long list; no one calls for orders, or solicits the favour of custom; no inviting circulars or enticing advertisements create an appetite for new purchases, and make one believe that superfluous things are absolutely necessary, and must be had. Nor does the husband go to town every day, and bring back anything the dear wife has forgotten. Her mental powers and good management must be equal to getting everything in before the winter arrives, not for the family only, but for the labourers also; and all this perhaps on slender means, sparse harvests, and bad seasons. In this respect, therefore, if for no other, the

betrothal system comes in well, affording the young couple plenty of time
for the acquisition of a thorough knowledge of what their new position may
necessitate.

There is one thing, however, Norwegians do not comprehend, and that
is the blessing of ventilation. They cannot understand it, and certainly
never practise it. Their rooms are stuffed up in every conceivable way.
As soon as the cold weather begins the internal atmosphere of the house

The Gentle Reproof.

remains unchanged until the following summer. When you open the door
you have to cut your way in ; it is as dense as cold turtle, and less agreeable. The marvel is that colds are not more prevalent, from the fact
that the good folk wash their necks on Saturday afternoon as a preparation for the Sunday, when they dress in their best, and look like different
creatures.

E are drawing near to the end of our tether, and much as we love home, there is not the same buoyancy about the return, however happy or successful the trip may have been, as there is about the start; for the latter is an important event, teeming with hope and expectancy, from the *couleur-de-rose* descriptions of friends who have preceded us, and who have heartily enjoyed the recapitulation of their adventures, narrow escapes, and temporary deprivations. But it is very different with the end of a journey. There is something of the Ichabod in it; and yet we know not why there should be; for if it has been one of danger, we ought to be thankful that it is over; and if, on the contrary, it has been productive of pleasant associations, we should still be thankful, inasmuch as it will prove a bright spot to fall back upon and refresh ourselves with when wearied in after-life. So we will not be depressed at the end of our trip to Gamle Norge; we would rather think of all the kindnesses of the people, the grand scenery of the coast, the combinations of sea-rock façade and snow, and learn a lesson of contentment and Christian love from the *bönder* and their happy families.

Having overcome this very natural feeling of regret that our holiday is over, let us, in conclusion, notice a few leading characteristics of the country which have been unnoted as we passed through it. Its geology is most characteristic, while in variety of climate it stands alone. Its wood-carving, too, has great individuality; and so has its old silver.*

* THE NEW CURRENCY OF NORWAY.—This change from the old specie dollar and skillings came into force on January 1st, 1877, when specie dollars, marks or orts, and skillings became matters of history. The new *régime* is as follows:—

KRONE AND ØRE.

SILVER. 1 krone = 30 skillings of old Norwegian money = 1s. 1¼d.
1 krone is divided into 100 öre.
Silver coins are 1 kroner. Copper coins are 1 öre, 2 öre, 5 öre.

Let us, then, take a general view of the geological formation. Any one specially interested in this subject should study the "Geologisk oversigtskart over det Sydlige Norge," 1858 to 1865, by Theodore Kjerulf og Tellef Dahll; but for others a general idea will suffice.

1. Gneiss predominates in the Romsdal and Sneehættan districts; also north and south of Sogne fjord, running down to the entrance of Hardanger.

2. Granite predominates in the south in large areas up to the Vöring Fos, and in detached portions in Vestranden towards Trondhjem. Christiansand is granite.

3. Sparagmit fjeldets (Norske) is found in Central Norway. This is a conglomerate of red sandstone, and sometimes called red and grey sparagmite.

4. Trondhjem quartz in the north, really hard schist: not found south of the Dovre fjeld.

5. Syenite and porphyry round Christiania.

6. Labrador stone occurs west of Lindernæs, in the south, at Ekersund on the west coast, below Stavanger, round the Galdhopiggen (the highest point in Norway), and north-east of Fortun, in the Sogne fjord.

The whole of this surface bears record of the immense extent and effect of the glacial period of Norway. The valleys show the glacial set as distinctly as does the tide in large rivers, the greatest attrition and scoriation being in the concaves going down. Huge bastions of rock * have been rounded and ground down by constant attrition, and vast terraces of sand, at the end of each valley, are the result of this attrition accumulating for ages. It would be very interesting to analyze and find the component parts of these immense deposits. Certain it is there is no

---

krone = 50 øre.
krone = 25 øre.
krone = 10 øre.

Gold Coins scarce; gold coins having been introduced only in 1875).

to kroner pieces and 20 kroner.

Notes. 5 kr., 10 kr., 25 kr., 50 kr., 100 kr., 500 kr., 1000 kr.

18 kroner = one sovereign English.

See the rocks of Steensand, on the west coast; these are conglomerate.

natural sandy soil above, and, as we have before mentioned, when reindeer-hunting, we have found huge boulders of thirty or forty feet at an
elevation of 5,000 feet, with smaller ones of a different formation resting
on them. Now all this has been brought about by the influence of the
gulf stream; when the gulf stream took this course the glacial period
ceased in Norway. That epoch none can tell. It will be sufficient to
notice the result, which is this: when the polar current from Spitzbergen
runs down the west coast of the Atlantic, and produces the great fogs off
Newfoundland, the gulf stream, driven up from the Gulf of Florida by
the force of the great caldron of the equator, strikes on to our west coast
and the coast of Norway, running up to the North Cape; in fact, the
only timber to be obtained there is the drift wood from the West Indies;
and at Hammerfest casks of palm oil have been washed up from Cape
Lopez Point, in Africa. In Iceland, too, as Professor Ericker Magnussen
informs us, the bridges are made of mahogany. Not that bridges are
frequent in that country; but those which they have are made from the
logs washed up there. This accounts for the variety of temperature which
the two boundaries of Norway—the gulf stream on the west, and Sweden
on the east—present. For instance, though Bergen and Christiania are
in about the same latitude, the average temperature at the former is
46° 8′ and at the latter 41° 5′; the summer average is about the same;
but in the winter months Christiania is often 13° colder than Bergen. Hence
there may be skating at Christiania while there is none at all at Bergen,
where the average annual rainfall is 72 inches, which, by the way, is lower
than that in our English lakes.

| | MEAN TEMPERATURE. | | | |
	Winter.	Spring.	Summer.	Autumn.
Christiania	+ 25	+ 38°	+ 60°	+ 42°
Bergen . .	+ 36	+ 45	+ 58°	+ 48
Trondhjem	+ 24	+ 35	+ 64	+ 40
North Cape .	+ 24	+ 30°	+ 42	+ 32

The mean temperature at North Cape is 32°, the greatest cold arising
from north-east winds. Thunder-storms occur in winter, while west winds
cause dense fogs.

At the conclusion of Forbes's " Norway " will be found a most interesting map, with isothermal lines passing through those places which have the same temperature in the months of January and July; and it is very

Stabio and Wooden Tankards.

striking to notice that the July temperature of the north of Ireland and Edinburgh is maintained through Norway as far as the Arctic Circle, when it begins to deflect to the eastward, where the gulf stream's influence ceases.

Again, the waterfalls are a great feature of this country. Some one has depicted Norway thus ⌐⌐⌐⌐⌐⌐, and the Alps thus ΛΛΛΛΛΛ. There is much truth in this. The valleys running down to the fjords produce immense precipices, down which rush the many waters of the high plateaux of 3,000 or 4,000 feet; and in some parts these falls are strengthened by the waters of the vast stretch of *snæbræden*, or snow-fields, of which the Justedal and the Folgefond are the most extensive.

The casual observer, looking at the map of Norway, would think it well populated, but a few years ago its inhabitants numbered hardly more than one-fourth those of London and its suburbs.* The names on the map frequently represent mere stations, farms, *prastegaarden*, or rectories, and villages are seldom seen. As in Scotland, the farmer takes the name of his land. In fact, Norway and Scotland are very closely allied to each other in many respects.

From the Runic downwards, the wood-carving of Norway stands alone for distinctive characteristics, and is still carried on in every variety by means of the simple national tolle-knife, which is ready for every-thing.

The lintels and carvings of the *staburs*, or store-houses, in Thelemarken have been already shown, but the most interesting specimens are found in churches, where the tortuous lines are full of originality and power of design. Serpents are ever-present and ever-varying, the museums being rich in specimens of this ecclesiastical class of work. Wood, and birch especially, is used for every kind of domestic utensil, and ornamentation is very generally introduced. Some of the old horse collars are beautiful, and are sometimes painted; tankards are richly carved; spoons profusely so; and on some occasions the bridegroom, if he be very expert, prepares a double spoon for the bride and himself, wherewith to eat their por-ridge simultaneously. Drinking bowls, salt-boxes, *mangel stoks*, are all carved; and this art is much encouraged by the long winter evenings.

The old silver of Norway is so large a subject that a series of illustra-

* Population of Norway, 1,150,000.

tions would be necessary to do justice to the matter; but its day is fast passing away. The peasants and fishermen have found new outlets for their earnings, and the time has gone by when they wondered what new thing they could have made in the precious metal; in fact, electro-plate is now invading Gamle Norge. May the *bönder* select the blessings of civilisation and eschew its evils! May their home happiness and love be ever-increasing, and the kind welcome which we have so often experienced never decrease in heartiness! For a time farewell!

FARVEL, FARVEL!

Costume of Lutheran Priest of Norway.